To: Roy
with ?
and go
Christian love... Basil Overton

6-17-05

MW01505539

A BOOK ABOUT

THE BOOK

BY

Basil Overton

© Copyright 2004

All rights reserved. No part of this publicationmay be reproduced, stored in a retrieval system, or transmitted in any form or by any means – electronic, mechanical, photocopy, recording, or otherwise – without prior permission of the copyright owner and Quality Publications.

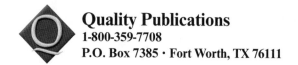

Quality Publications
1-800-359-7708
P.O. Box 7385 · Fort Worth, TX 76111

Basil Overton

Basil Overton was born to Raymond and Mary Overton in Weakley County, Tennessee December 3, 1925, where he grew up on farms with two brothers and three sisters. He served two years in the U.S. Navy during World War II. He has preached the gospel since 1945. He has done "local work" in a number of places, and worked in "mission" fields seventeen years. He has preached in about six hundred series of gospel meetings. He has spoken on lectureships of most of the colleges affiliated with churches of Christ.

Brother Overton is editor of The World Evangelist a gospel journal he started in 1972. He has been Vice President at Heritage Christian University (formerly International Bible College) since 1972, the year he started teaching there.

Basil has been married to the former Margie Medling since 1945. They have four children (one deceased), eight grandchildren, and one great grandchild.

Brother Overton attended Freed-Hardeman College (now University) 1946-1949, and was graduated with the highest honor conferred by the school. He attended Abilene Christian College (now University) two semesters. He has a B.A. Degree from Eastern Kentucky State University; an M.A. from the University of Kentucky; and a Doctor of Humanities Degree from Morehead State University.

Basil is the author of more than 50 gospel tracts, and the following other books: (1) What Happened To The Body; (2) Religious Discussion Notes; (3) Seven Score Short Sermons; (4) Evolution Or Creation?; (5) Evolution In The Light Of Scripture, Science, And Sense; (6) Conversions In Acts; (7) Mule Musings; (8) When Christ Was Preached To Christ And 51 Other Sermons; (9) The Highest Peak Of Human Performance (26 Sermons); and (10) Gems From Greek.

About 2,500 articles written by brother Overton have been published.

Basil Overton

**Freed Hardeman College
(now University) three years**

**Abilene Christian college
(now University) two semesters**

**B.A., Eastern Kentucky State
College (now University)**

M.A., University of Kentucky

**Doctor of Humanities,
Morehead State University**

4

Dedication

To my Margie's and my children:

Timothy (deceased); Gaius, Registered Architect;

Tessa, Registered Nurse; and Gretchen,

Registered Dental Hygenist

FOREWORD

Some time ago, Dr. Basil Overton mentioned to me that he was working on a new book entitled *A Book About The Book*. I was immediately intrigued, because I knew that coming from Basil Overton it would be a gem. Since that time I have asked him several times, "When is *A Book About The Book* going to be ready?" I am so happy that he has been able to excavate some time from his busy schedule in order to complete this wonderful volume. I have just read *A Book About The Book*, and it is, as I knew it would be, a joy to read and packed with fascinating and helpful information.

Most people who know him recognize that brother Overton has a way of making technical details accessible and understandable to those of us who are not schooled in some of those areas of study. Plus, he does it in a way that makes it a joy to learn.

This work contains insights and information about the Book of books, the Bible. Brother Overton delves into Bible backgrounds, how the Bible made its journey from the first century, evidences of the Bible's inspiration, and other relevant topics, providing a treasure trove of sermon and Bible class material along the way.

Now that I have read it, I can hardly wait until it is published so that I can have my own copy. There is a great deal in it that was enlightening to me and that I want to use in my teaching and preaching. I think that you will find this to be the case as well. Is there a better recommendation for a book than that?

> Dr. Kippy Myers
> Chairman, Department of
> Interdisciplinary Studies
> Freed-Hardeman University
> Henderson, TN

INTRODUCTION

In His excellent book entitled, *I Love Books*, John D. Snider, says that on July 28, 1917, Woodrow Wilson, then President of the United States, wrote the following.

"The Bible is the word of life. I beg that you will read it and find this outfor yourselves – read, not little snatches here and there, but long passages that will really be the road to the heart of it.

"You will find it not only full of real men and women, but also of the things you have wondered about and been troubled about all your life, as men have been always; and the more you read, the more will it become plain to you the things that are worth while and what are not, what things make men happy – loyalty, right dealing, speaking the truth, readiness to give everything for what they think their duty, and, most of all, the wish that they may have the approval of the Christ, who gave everything for them; and the things that are guaranteed to make men unhappy – selfishness, cowardice, greed, and everything that is low and mean.

"When you have read the Bible you will know that it is the word of God, because you will have found it the key to your own heart, your own happiness, and your own duty."

It is refreshing to know that President Wilson knew that it was not blind acceptance to believe that the Bible is the word of God. Indeed, reason tells us it is easier to believe that, than it is to believe this Blessed Book is the word of man.

It is my heart's desire and prayer to God that *A Book About The Book* will enlighten and encourage many in their seeking the Lord and the way to Heaven.

I am indebted to my daughter, Tessa Beth Berryman for her faithful efforts of computer work in getting this book ready for the publisher

Basil Overton, Editor
The World Evangelist
P O Box 2279
Florence, AL 35630
May 29, 2003

TABLE OF CONTENTS

Chapter One

THE MEANING OF "BOOK" AND
SOME EARLY TRANSLATIONS OF THE BIBLE
AND CHAPTERS AND VERSES

A **Book About The Book** was designed by the author to generate more confidence in the Bible as the word of God. Christians need the comfort and encouragement of "the full assurance of faith." (Hebrews 10:22.) Perhaps many of those who are not Christians would become Christians if they had more assurance that the Bible is indeed the word of God. If one's faith starves it will be because he did not feed it. Soul saving faith comes by hearing the word of God. (Romans 10:17; John 20:30,31.) One can have assurance that the Bible is that word.

It may surprise some to learn that preachers of the early centuries A.D. did not have nice leather bound, compact Bibles like we have. The reason for this was that Bibles and other books were not made in those early centuries as they are now made.

This does not mean the Bible did not exist in the early centuries A.D. Even the 27 New Testament books which we have, existed then, and were recognized as the word of God and therefore authoritative. But they did not exist in book form as we know books, because making of books as we know them was not started until hundreds of years later.

"The cloak that I left at Troas with Carpus, when thou comest bring with thee, and the books, but especially the parchments." (2 Timothy 4:13.) Books of this verse is a translation of the Greek word biblia which at the time of Paul meant what we call scrolls. The singular form biblos originally referred to the inner bark of the papyrus plant. Because a sort of paper or material on which writing was done was made out of this inner bark, the sheet or scroll of writing material was called biblos. Then what was written was called biblos as in the case of a "bill of divorcement" (Mark 10:4) and a "writing of divorcement" (Matthew 5:31; 19:7) and "book of the generation." (Matthew 1:1.) "Bill," "writing," and "book" in these passages all are translations of biblos. The first word of the Greek New Testament is Biblos from which came the word Bible.

The Making Of Books

Until the 200's or 300's A.D. "books" were just scrolls which were usually rolled up. Manuscripts were written on sheets of papyrus, or animal skins called vellum. Sometime in the second or third century sheets of manuscripts were placed between two thin wooden boards and called codices. The next step in book making was the sewing of the boards and sheets together with cords. These sheets of manuscripts were handwritten because the printing press was not invented until 1453 by John Gutenberg in Germany.

Allegedly the Bible was the first book printed on Gutenberg's moveable type press. After his invention books of all kinds were printed cheaply and in large quantities. The making of books has flourished since then. Machine bookbinding was begun in the early 1800's.

"Uncials" And Cursives"

Scholars say the oldest known Greek manuscripts of the New Testament were written entirely with capital letters called "Uncials," or "inch long," which is obviously an exaggeration of the size of the letters. At Earl's School in Weakley County, TN we were told to call capital letters in English, "boxcar letters." The uncial Greek letters were used in copying the New Testament from about the 3rd Century to the 10th Century.

Beginning in the 9th Century Greek New Testaments were written with smaller letters called "Cursives." The cursives were used until Gutenberg invented a printing press in the 15th century. There are many more cursive ancient Greek New Testament manuscripts than those in uncials. Scholars say the uncial manuscripts do not have the words separated.

Early Translations

"The validity of the Gospel revelation was, even before the end of the first century, submitted to the general consideration of mankind. Nearly the whole of the Scriptures was before that period translated into Latin, a language so well and so extensively known as to be understood even in the remotest parts of the Roman Empire. The reception of these sacred books at a period when from their recent dates the truth of every circumstance might be without difficulty ascertained, is one among the numerous proofs of the truth of the

Gospel." (James Smith, *History of The Christian Church*, page 58. My copy was published in 1835.)

I take Dr. Smith's statement to mean that most of the 27 books of the New Testament had been translated from Greek into Latin by the end of the first century A.D. The apostle John wrote the Book of Revelation near the end of the first century A.D. It may not have been translated that soon.

According to McClintock and Strong the Peshito Syriac translation of the Bible was an authorized version. They and other scholars say the New Testament part of it was translated in the second century. Some scholars say it was not completed in the second century but completed many years later.

The Old Syriac and the Old Latin translations of the New Testament were made about 150 A.D.

In his book, *Early Versions Of The New Testament*, Dr. Bruce Metzger of Princeton Theological Seminary says five or six versions of the New Testament were made in the Syriac language during the first six centuries of the Christian era. He thinks this is significant testimony concerning the vitality and scholarship of Syrian churchmen of those centuries.

Dr. Metzger also says that the distinguished scholar Eberhard Nestle says that no others of the early church did more than Syrians for the translating of the Bible into their language, and that there are in European libraries old Syriac Bible manuscripts from Lebanon, Egypt, Sinai, Mesopotamia, Armenia, India, and even China!

Dr. Eberhard Nestle produced an excellent Greek text of the New Testament. It was incorporated into a good Greek-English Interlinear New Testament by Dr. Alfred Marshall. I have a copy of it at home, and one in my office.

A scholar named Tatian was one of the students of the famous Justin Martyr in Rome. He returned to the East in 172 A.D. He wrote a *Harmony of the Gospels* that was circulated in Syria.

The great Christian scholar of the second century whose name was Origen gave a full list of all the 27 books of the New Testament. So did Eusebius another great scholar about 100 years later.

The fact that the New Testament scriptures were translated into several other languages so early in the Christian Era is obvious evidence those scriptures not only existed then but were recognized as being very important.

Chapters And Verses

The chapters and verses divisions as they are in our English Bibles were not always in the Bible. They are a great blessing in our studying and teaching the Bible. The history of how and when the chapters and verses were put in the Bible is much too complex and complicated for it all to be presented here.

Before the Old Testament books were divided into chapters, the Jews had made rather large divisions in some books. The chapter divisions were made in the 13th century in the Latin Bible. Some say Cardinal Hugo de St. Caro did this monumental work. Others say Stephen Langton did it.

Scholars say the Jews made verse divisions in the Hebrew text of the Old Testament at a very early date.

The oldest chapter divisions of Greek texts of the New Testament are in the Codex Vaticanus which dates to the fourth century A.D. In this manuscript of the New Testament there are 170 chapters in the Book of Matthew; sixty-chapters in Mark's account of Christ; 152 in Luke, and fifty in John. This does not mean the contents of these books are different to that in our New Testaments, it just means the chapter divisions are more frequent.

In Codex Alexandrinus which dates to the fifth century A.D. there are sixty-eight chapters in Matthew; forty-eight in Mark; eighty-three in Luke; and eighteen in John.

In no case in these ancient manuscripts of the New Testament does the first chapter stand at the beginning of a book, but in each there is an opening section known in Greek as the prooimion or preface. (See: Bruce M. Metzger, *The Test Of The New Testament*, Second Edition, Oxford University Press, page 22.)

Verse divisions were first made in Robert Stephens Greek New Testament in 1551. His son, Henry reported that his father did the work while on a journey on horseback from Paris to Lyons in France. (See *International Standard Bible Encyclopedia*, Vol. I, page 142.)

The first English version of the New Testament that was divided into verses was published in England during the reign of Queen Mary whose reign began in 1553. These verse divisions were arranged as Sir Robert Stephens arranged them in a Greek New Testament in 1551.

John Wycliffe, "the great reformer" was the first to translate the whole Bible into the English language. He translated it from the Latin

Vulgate version which was a translation from Hebrew and Greek in the fourth and fifth centuries. It took Wycliffe twenty-two years to translate the whole Bible into English. He used the chapter divisions Cardinal Hugo used in his Latin Bible in 1250. (For some of the foregoing facts see: Sidney Collett, *All About The Bible*, Fleming H. Revel Co., pages 32-38.)

Concerning early Egyptian versions of the New Testament, Dr. A. Berkeley Mickelesen, says, "The Egyptian or Coptic versions consist of a half-dozen or more varieties of the Old Egyptian tongue. Sahidic was the dialect of upper Egypt, Bohairic of lower Egypt. Between these two extremes were intermediate dialects, such as Fayumic, Memphitic, Achmimic, and sub-Achmimic. It is significant that every dialect group of people wanted the New Testament in their particular dialect." He also says, "The earliest Egyptian translation was made about A.D. 200." (*Can I Trust My Bible: Important Questions Often Asked About The Bible, With Some Answers By Eight Evangelical Scholars*; Moody Bible Institute of Chicago, 1966, page 159. Dr. Mickelesen is listed as Professor of Bible and Theology of the Wheaton College Graduate School.)

A more recent book says it is likely that various books of the Bible had been translated into Coptic by the second half of the third century. This book also contains much detailed information about the New Testament scriptures being gradually translated into all the Coptic dialects named above, through the third and fourth centuries. (Frederic Wisse: *The Text Of The New Testament In Contemporary Research*, Edited by Bart D. Erhman and Michael W. Holes; William B. Eerdmans Publishing Company; 1995; pages 131-139. This book was dedicated to Dr. Bruce M. Metzger for his 80th birthday, February 9, 1994.)

"Book, Chapter And Verse Preaching"

I have heard preachers talk considerably about the "urgency and importance of book, chapter, and verse preaching." Some writing has also been done on this subject.

Some have left the impression that they mean by "book, chapter, and verse preaching" the kind where the preacher states the book, chapter, and verse (or verses) where each of his quotations from the Bible is found. There certainly is nothing wrong with doing this. I have done it in all my 58 years of preaching! However, to say that a gospel preacher is unfaithful if he does not give the book, chapter and verse (or verses) every time he quotes scripture is a false charge.

One who does not really want emphasize God's word in his preaching, might recite very few Bible scriptures and he might fail to give the book, chapter, and verse references. But it is wrong to discredit a gospel preacher or his preaching merely because he does not always give book, chapter and verse, or verses for what he recites.

Jesus and the inspired writers and spokesmen did not give book, chapter and verse when they quoted Old Testament scriptures. Perhaps, what was nearest to doing this in the New Testament is Paul's saying, "as it is also written in the second Psalm," etc. (Acts 13:33.) But evidently the Holy Spirit did not feel it was an urgent matter to give the reference for a scripture quotation, for Paul then quoted from David and said what he quoted was in another psalm, and did not even tell which psalm it was! (Acts 13:35.)

It is contended by some that the reason Jesus and New Testament writers did not give "book chapter and verse or verses" is that at that time the books of the Old Testament had not been divided into chapters and verses. However, because of Paul's reference to "the second Psalm," and "another Psalm" in Acts 13:33,35, it is evident that some of, or all of, the 150 psalms had been numbered at that time. Maybe they had not been divided into verses.

The oldest of the approximately 6000 ancient Greek manuscripts of the New Testament that have been found do not even have the words separated. Centuries passed before the New Testament books were divided into chapters and verses. It is obvious that those who preached the New Testament Scriptures during those many years, did not cite "chapter and verse, or verses!" If they were "unsound" it was not because they did cite "book, chapter, and verse!"

We have enough problems with which to deal without making up things to bind, and perhaps cause dissension. It is certainly all right to cite chapters and verses in preaching, but let us not cause dissension by saying if a preacher does not always do this he is not faithful. We can lose credibility by trying to bind what is not bound by Holy Scripture!

Ways Jesus And Inspired Writers Cited
Statements From The Old Testament

1. They Used Names Of The Prophets. Jesus and inspired spokesmen and writers sometimes named in the New Testament the

prophets from whom they quoted, but did not give chapter and verse references. Examples of such are in the following passages: Matthew 2:17; 3:3; 4:14; 13:14; 15:7; 24:15; John 12: 38,39,41; Acts 1:25; Romans 10:16,20; 11:9.

2. "It Is Writtten." Many times quotations are prefaced by "It is written." Examples are in the following passages: Matthew 4:4,7,10; 26:24; Luke 24:46; John 12:14. Also "It is written in the prophets," prefaces some quotations as in John 6:45. In none of these were book, chapter, and verse given!

3. "The Scripture Was Fulfilled." Sometimes quotations are prefaced by "The scripture was fulfilled" as in Mark 15:28 and John 19:26. Also by "That the scripture might be fulfilled which the Holy Ghost by the mouth of," and then the prophet is named. (Acts 1:16.) In none of these was chapter and verse or verses given.

"That the saying might be fulfilled" is another way scripture references are given. (John 18:9.)

4. "As It Is Written In The Law." Quotations are prefaced by "As it is written I the law of the Lord," as in Luke 2:23. No book, chapter, and verse was given.

5. "As It Is Written In The Book Of The Words Of." Some recitations of Old Testament scriptures are accompanied with "It is written in the book of the words of," and then the prophet's name is given as in Luke 3:4, but no chapter and verse.

6. "As It Was In The Days." Old Testament Scripture facts are recited by reference to a person and his times as in Luke 17:26, and no book, chapter, and verse was given.

7. "The Holy Ghost Said." The writers of the Old Testament were inspired or directed by the Holy Ghost. (2 Peter 1:21.) This accounts for the statements in the New Testament that say in one way or another that the Holy Ghost said things that are quoted from the Old Testament. Examples are in Acts 1:16; 28:25; Hebrews 3:7; 9:8.

8. "Spoken By God." Something recorded in the Old Testament is referred to as something spoken by God as in Matthew 22:32, but no book, chapter, and verse is given.

The foregoing should be abundant evidence that reciting book, chapter, and verse when quoting what the Bible says is merely a convenience for auditors and readers, but not compulsory in order for one to be a faithful preacher, otherwise Jesus and the inspired spokesmen and writers were not faithful!

There are enough things for us to oppose and about which to be concerned without making up superficial matters to fight.

"Beloved, when I gave all diligence to write unto you of the common salvation, it was needful for me to write unto you, and exhort you that ye should earnestly contend for the faith once delivered unto the saints." (Jude 3.)

Questions And Discussion Points

1. Explain why preachers of the early centuries A.D. did not have Bibles in the form of ours.

2. What did Paul want Timothy to bring to him?

3. Explain how the word Bible came to be.

4. Discuss "bill," "writing," and "book" in Mark 10:4; Matthew 5:31; 19:7; 1:1.

5. What was the first kind of book making?

6. Who invented the printing press, and when?

7. Discuss early translations of the New Testament.

8. Do you think you appreciate the Bible being in such neat and convenient form as you have it?

Chapter Two

THE OLD TESTAMENT CANON

The Assyrian word **ganu** and the Hebrew word **ganeh** meant reed, or tube. Evidently these developed into Greek **kanna** and Latin **canna**. The English word <u>cane</u> came from this word. Also, the English word canon came from it. Measuring sticks, like our yard-sticks, were made from reeds or canes. So a canon was a measuring stick or line, or rule.

The writings admitted into the Bible were admitted because they were measured by the rule that the ones who wrote them were guided by God Almighty in what they wrote. Therefore these writings were measured or canonized. They constituted the sacred canon. So the sacred canon just means the Holy Scriptures, or what we know as the 66 books of the Bible. These constitute the inspired word of God.

They Had Credentials

It was not difficult to determine whether or not the writers of the Bible wrote words which were given to them by God, or which were inspired of God. This is true of Old Testament as well as New Testament writings.

Peter said the Spirit of Christ was in the Old Testament prophets which enabled them to write things which they wrote. (1 Peter 1:10-12.) Peter also said that the Holy Ghost moved the Old Testament prophets to say what they said. (2 Peter 1:21.)

The Spirit of Christ being in the Old Testament prophets, and their being moved by the Holy Ghost were demonstrated with visions; interpretations of dreams; escaping terrible situations like Daniels' not being hurt in a den of lions; miracles and wonders like the dividing of the Red Sea; water being turned to blood; a rod being turned into a serpent as in the case of Moses; and in various other ways.

There were signs, wonders and mighty deeds wrought by the power of God in and through New Testament writers. (2 Corinthians 12:12.) Some tried to convince Christians in Ephesus that they were apostles. They were tried and proven to be liars. (Revelation 3:1,2.) These impostors were a bold contrast to those who were really guided by the Holy Spirit who had divine demonstrations and credentials to prove they were!

God does not will to perform miracles now. Miracles were confined to the times when God was revealing his will and having it written in His Holy Scriptures, the Bible. But, if God were now to perform miracles through men, and two men were to come into your community, both claiming that God was directing them in what they spoke and wrote, and one could perform miracles like changing water to blood, changing walking sticks into snakes, walking on water, raising people from the dead, and replacing missing arms, legs, or other body parts, and performing other such miracles, and the other man could not do such, which one would you accept as being inspired of, or directed by God in what he said? Of course your answer would be, "The one who could perform the miracles."

So, it was easy for people to know what books measured up, and should be admitted into the sacred canon, or the Holy Bible.

Yes, indeed, each case of inspiration in the Old Testament and in the New Testament was measured by valid credentials. So it was easy for people to know what books measured up and should be admitted into the Sacred Canon, or the Holy Bible.

What Others Have Written

Flavius Josephus was a Jewish historian who lived when Jesus and his apostles lived. He wrote some concerning the Old Testament Scriptures. What he refers to as 22 books are exactly the same as the 39 books in our Old Testament. In the Jewish Canon of Scripture 1 and 2 Samuel were one book; so with 1 and 2 Kings; so with 1 and 2 Chronicles. What we call the Twelve Minor Prophets constituted one book. Other books were also combined in the Jewish Sacred Canon of the Old Testament so that their 22 books are exactly the same as the 39 books in our Old Testament. It is said the Jews arranged the Old Testament into 22 books because of the 22 letters of the Hebrew alphabet.

Here is something Josephus wrote about the Old Testament Canon. "...because every one is not permitted of his own accord to be a writer, nor is there any disagreement in what is written; they being only prophets that have written the original and earliest accounts of things as they learned them of God himself by inspiration; and others have written what hath happened in their own times, and that in a very distinct manner also.

"For we have not an innumerable multitude of books among us, disagreeing from, and contradicting one another (as the Greeks have),

24

but only twenty-two books, which contain the records of all the past times; which are justly believed to be divine; and of them five belong to Moses, which contain his laws and the traditions of the origin of mankind, till his death. This interval of time was little short of 3000 years; but as to the time from the death of Moses till the reign of Artaxerxes, king of Persia, who reigned after Xerxes, the prophets, who were after Moses, wrote down what was done in their times in thirteen books. The remaining four books contain hymns to God, and precepts for the conduct of human life. It is true, our history hath been written since Artaxerxes very particularly, but hath not been esteemed of the like authority with the former by our forefathers, because there hath not been an exact succession of prophets since that time; and how firmly we have given credit to those books of our own nation, is evident by what we do; for, during so many ages as have already passed, no one has been so bold as either to add any thing to them, to take any thing from them, or to make any change in them; but it becomes natural to all Jews, immediately and from their very birth, to esteem those books to contain divine doctrines, and to persist in them, and, if occasion be, willing to die for them. For it is no new thing for our captives, many of them in number, and frequently in time, to be seen to endure racks and deaths of all kinds upon the theatres, that they may not be obliged to say one word against our laws and the records that contain them...." (*The Works of Josephus*, The S.S. Scranton Company, 1919, page 885.)

Dr. William Henry Green of Princeton Theological Seminary was a great Bible Apologist. He defended the Bible as being the word of God. Concerning the 39 books of the Old Testament, Dr. Green wrote: "No formal declaration of their canonicity was needed to give them sanction. They were from the first not only eagerly read by the devout, but also believed to be divinely obligatory. Each individual book of an acknowledged prophet of Jeh, or of anyone accredited as inspired by him to make known his will, was accepted as the Word of God immediately upon its appearance.... Those books and those only were accepted as the Divine standards of their faith, and regulative of their conduct which where written for this definite purpose by those whom they believed to be inspired of God." (Dr. W. H. Green, *International Standard Bible Encyclopedia*, Vol. 1, page 554.)

Jeh in the quotation from Dr. Green is a form of the Hebrew word for God. The distinguished scholar, Gleason L. Archer wrote: "The only true test of canonicity which remains is the testimony of God the Holy Spirit to the authority of His own Word. This testimony found a response of recognition, faith, and submission in the hearts of God's people who walked in covenant fellowship with Him. As E. J. Young puts it, 'To these and other proposed criteria we must reply with a negative. The canonical books of the Old Testament were divinely revealed and their authors were holy men who spoke as they were borne of the Holy Ghost. In His good providence God brought it about that His people should recognize and receive His Word. How He planted this conviction in their hearts with respect to the identity of His Word we may not be able fully to understand or explain. We may, however, follow our Lord, who placed the imprimatur of His infallible authority upon the books of the Old Testament.' (E. J. Young, *The Canon of the Old Testament, in Revelation and the Bible*, p. 168.)

"We may go further than this and point out that in the nature of the case we could hardly expect any other valid criteria than this. If canonicity is a quality somehow imparted to the books of Scripture by any kind of human decision, as Liberal scholars unquestioningly assume (and as even the Roman Church implies by her self-contradictory affirmation: 'The Church is the mother of the Scripture'), then perhaps a set of mechanical tests could be set up to determine which writings to accept as authoritative and which to reject. But if, on the other hand, a sovereign God has taken the initiative in revelation and in the production of an inspired record of that revelation through human agents, it must simply be a matter of recognition of the quality already inherent by divine act in the books so inspired. When a child recognizes his own parent from a multitude of other adults at some public gathering, he does not impart any new quality of parenthood by such an act; he simply recognizes a relationship which already exists. So also with lists of authoritative books drawn up by ecclesiastical synods or councils. They did not impart canonicity to a single page of Scripture: they simply acknowledged the divine inspiration of religious documents which were inherently canonical from the time they were first composed, and formally rejected other books for which canonicity had been falsely claimed." (Gleason L. Archer, *A Survey Of Old Testament Introduction*, pages 85,86.)

Questions And Discussion Points

What is the purpose of this book?

What does canon mean? Discuss.

What does Sacred Canon mean?

Discuss why it was easy to determine who was inspired, and who was not guided by God. Discuss 2 Corinthians 12:12.

Discuss the part about two men coming into a community.

Who was Flavius Josephus? What was he?

Discuss what Josephus wrote about the Old Testament Canon.

Discuss what Dr. W. H. Green wrote about the Old Testament books.

Chapter Three

MORE ON THE OLD TESTAMENT CANON

The Septuagint As Evidence

Alexander the Great died in 320 B.C. after conquering a vast amount of territory. He spread Greek culture into the Hebrew world and into the Persian culture. After his death his vast kingdom was divided into three parts by 275 B.C. These were: (1) Macedon and Greece which were ruled by Antiogonus; (2) Seleucid, Syria, and Persia, which were ruled by Seleucus; and (3) Egypt was ruled by the Ptolemies.

Ptolemy Philadephius or Ptolemy II, was one of the rulers of Egypt. The Greek language and culture had so influenced the Hebrew world that Ptolemy II inaugurated the translating of the Hebrew Old Testament Scriptures into the Greek language. This was done in Alexandria, Egypt the city named after Alexander the Great.

This great work of translating the Hebrew Old Testament into Greek is said to have begun in 270 B.C. Apparently 70 scholars started this great work. This is why the translation is called The Septuagint, because this name means seventy. One tradition says the translation was completed in 70 or 72 days by 72 Palestinian Jews. (*New World Dictionary of the American Language.*) Others indicate many years went by before the Septuagint was completed.

The Septuagint is great evidence that not only did the Old Testament exist in the third century B.C., it was also recognized by the highest officials and authorities as being a very important book. Some have said the Septuagint was the first book of any note to be translated.

By the time the Septuagint translation was begun, the Old Testament was a well established and recognized collection of writings which had been measured by the rule that their writers were directed by the Lord. They were divinely directed! They had divine credentials. They could perform miracles by the power of the God who guided them in what they wrote!

Most of the passages from the Old Testament which are recited in the New Testament are from the Septuagint.

The Jews

At the time Jesus was on earth the Jewish people had many traditions. These traditions were very important to them. They were later written in such works as the Talmud and the Targums. The traditions known as the Talmud were first written by Rabbi Judah Hakkadosh (Judah the Holy). He was born in 135 A.D. He wrote the text of the Talmud known as Mishna in the 2nd century A.D.

It is very difficult to determine when the Jewish Targums were written. Some think they were written in the 2nd century A.D. also. Targum means to translate or to explain somewhat like what was done according to Nehemiah chapter eight in the Old Testament.

Webster says the Targums are "any of several translations or paraphrases of parts of the Hebrew Scriptures, written in the vernacular (Aramaic) of Judea."

The Interpreter's Bible says the Targums are the Aramaic translation of scriptural books, especially the Penteteuch (first five books of the Old Testament), as delivered orally in the synagogues during the period of the second temple and later, in accordance with a generally accepted, but by no means rigidly fixed, tradition of interpretation.

I have written the foregoing to emphasize that even though the Jews at the time of Jesus had strong feelings about certain oral traditions, interpretations, etc., they did not allow any of these to be a part of the Sacred Canon of the Old Testament Scriptures.

Jesus often rebuked some of the Jews because they let their traditions keep them from doing God's will. "But he answered and said unto them, why do ye also transgress the commandment of God by your tradition? For God commanded, saying, Honour thy father and thy mother: and, He that curseth father or mother, let him die the death. But ye say, whosoever shall say to his father or his mother, it is a gift, by whatsoever thou mightest be profited by me: and honor not his father and his mother, he shall be free. Thus have ye made the commandment of God of none effect by your tradition. Ye hypocrites, well did Esaias prophesy of you saying, This people draweth nigh to me with their mouth, and honoureth me with their lips; but their heart is far from me. But in vain they do worship me, teaching for doctrines the commandments of men." (Matthew 15:3-9.)

"Howbeit in vain do they worship me, teaching for doctrines the commandments of men. For laying aside the commandment of God, ye hold the tradition of men, as the washing of pots and cups: and many other such things ye do. And he said unto them, Full well ye reject the commandment of God, that ye may keep your own tradition." (Mark 7:7-9.)

Yes, Jesus rebuked the Jews many times for their following traditions instead of God's word, but our Lord never even hinted that the Jews had corrupted the Sacred Canon of the Old Testament Scriptures! Jesus censured the Jews for not obeying the Sacred Scriptures, and for misrepresenting them, and for rendering the Holy Scriptures void by their traditions, but there is no evidence our Saviour ever accused the Jews of adding anything to the text of the Old Testament Canon!

There is no indication that there was ever any controversy between Jesus and the Jews over his reference to the Old Testament Scriptures, and he referred to them and quoted from them many times as in Matthew 26:54; 22:29; Mark 14:49; John 5:39; 10:35.

The Jews disagreed on many matters, but generally they agreed on what books ought to be in the Old Testament, and those were the 39 books which are in our Old Testament!

What Many Attacks On The Old Testament Canon Prove!

This is a big subject and space forbids anything but a brief summary of it here.

In many centuries there were negative critics of the Old Testament Canon. In his book: *Introduction To The Old Testament*, published by William B. Eerdmans in Grand Rapids, MI in 1971, Dr. R. K. Harrison presents the names of many of these critics. He was Professor of Old Testament in Wycliffe College of the University of Toronto. I gleaned some of the following information from his book and put it in my own words.

Attacks on the Old Testament were made in the first Century A.D. The Gnostics were negative critics of it in the Second Century A.D. This means the Old Testament was there and the critics made it obvious it had been in existence a long time. Valentinus of Alexandria, Egypt was one of the prominent Gnostic leaders that made an assault on it in the Second Century.

An infidel named Celsus began his efforts against the Old Testament in the latter part of the Second Century. He wrote a treatise entitled <u>A True Word</u> about 180 A.D. He showed in this treatise that he had only a slight acquaintance with Old Testament history and religion in general.

Dr. E. W. Hengtenberg (1802-1869) a superb classical scholar, specialized in Old Testament studies in Berlin, Germany. In scholarly circles he had the reputation of being a fierce foe of rationalism and challenger of religious liberalism. He was a prolific writer in German, and some of his works were translated into English.

Negative critics of the Bible have caused it to shine even more brilliantly. It is like a stone that is rubbed; the more it is rubbed, the brighter it shines.

A very able Christian apologist or defender of the Word of God named Origen refuted *A True Word* with a document entitled: *Contra Celsum*. Celsus and Origen also conducted a debate by correspondence in which Celsus quoted at least 80 passages from the New Testament in efforts to get around what they said!

All this proves that in the Second and Third Centuries A.D. the Old Testament and the New Testament were both alive and well and annoyed those who did not accept them as the Word of God!

Why did not Celsus and the other negative critics of the Bible just ignore it? Obviously they knew the Bible was well received as from God and authorative, and all this was a serious problem for them indeed! The flimsy attacks of those critics and others like them during many centuries prove that the word of God has endured the teeth of time! Dr. Harrison lists many negative critics of the Bible in many centuries and comments that the Old Testament Canon has survived all of them!

Dr. Harrison says that to Celsus belongs the dubious distinction of assembling most of the arguments which have been made against Christianity and the Bible by subsequent generations of rationalists, atheists, and agnostics!

Questions And Discussion Points

Discuss Alexander the Great.

What is the Septuagint?

Who ordered the making of the Septuagint?

What bearing does the Septuagint have on the Canon of the Old Testament? Discuss.

What is the Talmud? Who wrote the text of it?

What are the Targums?

Have the Jews made the Talmud and/or the Targums a part of the Sacred Canon of the Old Testament?

Did Jesus accuse the Jews of adding anything to the Sacred Canon of the Old Testament? Discuss.

Chapter Four

JESUS CHRIST AND THE HOLY GHOST ON THE OLD TESTAMENT CANON

Jesus Christ was well aware of the Canon of the Old Testament. The Old Testament which he used contained the 22 books which the Jews recognized as the divine books which were the same as the 39 books in our Old Testament.

There is no indication that Jesus differed with the Jews over what writings should be in the Old Testament. So, our blessed Savior is the greatest of all witnesses concerning the Sacred Canon of the Old Testament Scriptures.

My sons and I had the rare privilege of hearing the late Dr. Edward J. Young lecture at Asbury Seminary in Wilmore, KY about 1965. We visited with him for a while. He was Professor of Old Testament at Westminster Theological Seminary in Philadelphia, PA. He was recognized as one of the best scholars in the world on the Old Testament. His book, *An Introduction To The Old Testament* is a classic. On page 38 he wrote concerning Christ and the other Jews of His time that there is no evidence whatever of any dispute between Him and the Jews about the Canonicity of any Old Testament book. He said what concerned Christ was not the Old Testament canon which they accepted, but the oral traditions by which they made that canon void. (Matthew 15:8.)

There is no evidence that those Jews contended that their traditions were a part of that canon!

Obviously, our Lord did not refer to the New Testament Scriptures when he referred to, or quoted from the Scriptures, because the New Testament was not written until after he ascended back to heaven. We know, therefore, that Jesus referred to, and quoted from, the very same Old Testament Scriptures which we have. I do not mean that Jesus had the Old Testament Scriptures in the English language, for the English language did not come into existence until many hundreds of years after Jesus was on earth.

Jesus Christ Used The Scriptures Of The Old Testament
Not only was Jesus well aware of the same Old Testament books which we have, he also relied on them heavily.

1. Jesus recognized the Old Testament Scriptures as the word of God. (Mark 7:8-12.)

2. The same text indicates that Jesus recognized the Old Testament Scriptures as authorative, and that those who lived under them were refusing to submit to God's authority if they did not follow them.

3. Jesus taught that what was written by Moses was what was spoken by God. (Matthew 22:31,32.)

4. When our Lord was confronted by the arch-fiend of mankind, the Devil himself, he quoted Old Testament Scriptures to overcome the temptations. (Matthew 4.)

5. The Savior used Old Testament Scriptures to expose the errors of the Sadducees. (Matthew 22:29-32.)

6. The Lord appealed to Old Testament Scriptures as examples of warning as in the case of Lot's wife. (Luke 17:32.)

7. The Savior referred a lawyer to the Old Testament Scriptures to find the answer to his question concerning eternal life. (Luke 10:25,26.)

8. Jesus used Old Testament Scripture to prove his Messiahship. (John 5:45-47.) He said Moses wrote concerning him.

9. Isaiah in the Old Testament prophesied regarding the unbelief of the Jews who lived when Christ was on earth, and the Lord said he did. (Matthew 13:14,15.)

Differences In The Old And The New

Our Saviour was born under the law of Moses. (Galatians 4:4.) He taught the Jews to live by the law of Moses. (Matthew 23:1-3.) This was because they were living under that law and it was God's law for them. This was before Jesus died and took that law out of the way, and abolished it, and gave the new covenant.

When Jesus Christ died on Calvary he abolished the law of Moses. (Colossians 2:14; Ephesians 2:14-16; Romans 7:4; 2 Corinthians 3:7-11.) His new covenant did not come into force until after his death. (Hebrews 9:15-17.)

There are two extremes regarding the Old Testament. One is the view that we can learn how to be Christians and how to worship God from the Old Testament. The other is that the Old Testament is of no value at all to us.

The Old Testament helps us to understand the New Testament. Paul referred to the Old Testament when he wrote that what was written therein was written for our learning. (Romans 15:4.)

There are great examples of faith, and also sad examples of unfaithfulness and disobedience in the Old Testament.

There are great principles stated in the Old Testament which never change. But we cannot learn from the Old Testament how to become Christians and how to worship and serve God in the church. These things we have to learn from the new covenant in the New Testament.

Things The Holy Ghost Said

Peter wrote to Christians, "We have also a more sure word of prophecy; whereunto ye do well that ye take heed, as unto a light that shineth in a dark place, until the day dawn, and the day star arise in your hearts: knowing this first, that no prophecy of the scripture is of any private interpretation. For the prophecy came not in old time by the will of man: but holy men of God spake as they were moved by the Holy Ghost." (2 Peter 1:19-21.)

Officials of the Catholic Church misuse this text when they use it to support the idea that people cannot interpret the scriptures, but that they must rely on an official of the Catholic Church to do this for them. This is ironic because such a view is an obvious misinterpretation of this passage.

The context of the passage and also the original text make if obvious that "no prophecy of the scripture is of any private interpretation" means that what any prophet in the Old Testament wrote did not come from the prophet's own interpretation of what was presented to his mind, for what he said was what the Holy Ghost said through him.

What The Holy Ghost Said

Not only did Jesus Christ recognize the Old Testament books we have, and quote from them as God's word, also he and others in the New Testament affirmed that what the Old Testament says was said by the Holy Ghost.

1. "And Jesus answered and said, while he taught in the temple, How say the scribes that Christ is the son of David? For David himself said by the Holy Ghost, The Lord said to my Lord, Sit thou on

my right hand, till I make thine enemies thy footstool." (Mark 12:35,36.) Clearly, Jesus declared that what David said in Psalm 110:1 was really said by the Holy Ghost. One cannot really accept and believe the New Testament as an inspired book without also believing the Old Testament was produced by the Holy Ghost.

2. Peter said, "Men and brethren, this scripture must needs have been fulfilled which the Holy Ghost by the mouth of David spake before concerning Judas, which was guide to them that took Jesus. For he was numbered with us, and had obtained part of this ministry." (Acts 1:16,17.) Peter affirmed that what David said in Psalm 41:9 was really said by the Holy Ghost.

3. According to Luke in Acts 28:25-27, Paul told some Jews something Esaias had written in chapter six of his Old Testament book and Paul said concerning it, "Well spake the Holy Ghost by Esaias the prophet unto our fathers...." The Holy Ghost directed what New Testament writers wrote about how that what the Old Testament said was said by the Holy Ghost!

4. The writer of the New Testament book of Hebrews affirmed that what David and Jeremiah wrote in the Old Testament was actually said by the Holy Ghost. (Hebrews 3:7-11; 10:15-17.)

A Reliable Canon

The Sacred Canon of the Old Testament Scriptures is God's account of his great work of creation and of his dealings with his people.

The great Bible Apologist, James Smith dealt with some notable skeptics, one of whom was a Mr. Olmstead. The following is a sample of Mr. Smith's handling of Mr. Olmstead, and is an excellent statement that magnifies the reliability of the Old Testament.

"Mr. Olmstead enquires, 'How did Moses know what transpired at the creation?' To this it is replied, that it will be admitted this cosmogony of his was a mere vague tradition, and consequently unworthy of credit, provided it can be proved that it contains any error concerning the material world.

"But it is maintained that while all the false theologies of both the ancients and the moderns, abound not only with systems revolting in their views of the Deity, but with the grossest physical errors, that nothing of this nature is to be found in the writings of Moses, or in any of the books of the Bible.

"Had Moses, like the authors of the sacred writings of the Hindu. represented the moon as 50,000 leagues higher than the sun, that it shines by its own light, that it animates our body; that the night is formed by the descent of the sun behind the Someyra mountains, situated in the middle of the globe, and many thousand leagues high; that our earth is flat and triangular, composed of seven stories, each of which has its own degree of beauty, its inhabitants and its sea; that the first is of honey, the other is of sugar, the other of butter, the other of wine; and finally, that all the mass is carried on the heads of innumerable elephants, who in shaking themselves cause the earthquake, then we should have been brought to the mortifying conclusion that Moses was an impostor. Or had his writings contained one of the many errors with which those of the most eminent philosophers of Greece and Rome abound; or had he like Mohammed represented mountains as being made to hinder the earth from being moved, and represented it as being held by anchors and cords; or had he reasoned against the theory of antipodes, **we should have been constrained to have treated his natural philosophy with contempt, and as a consequence, would have spurned his theology**.

"But we rejoice under the conviction that not one of the sacred writers of the Bible, from the admirable Moses, who wrote in the desert four hundred years before the Trojan war, down to that fisherman, the son of Zebedee, who wrote in Ephesus and Patmos, during the reign of Domitian, not one of them have made one of those mistakes, which the science of every age discovers in the books of the preceding ages: none of those absurdities which modern astronomy discovers in such great numbers in the writings of the ancients."

The foregoing is from page 49 of a book this writer owns which was published in 1843 by James Smith, entitled: *The Christian's Defence*.

Questions And Discussion Points

1. Of what Canon of the Old Testament was Jesus aware?

2. Did Jesus argue with the Jews over what books should be in the Old Testament?

3. How is Jesus the greatest witness regarding the Old Testament Canon?

4. Explain why Jesus did not have an English Old Testament.

Discuss "private interpretation" of 2 Peter 1:19-21.

Did Jesus teach that what the Old Testament says was said by the Holy Ghost?

Discuss Mark 12:35,36.

Can one believe the New Testament is an inspired book without accepting the Old Testament as an inspired book?

Chapter Five

THOSE EXTRA BOOKS
IN SOME OLD TESTAMENTS

In some Bibles in the Old Testament section there is a group of books called the Apocrypha. "**Apocrypha**" is from the Greek "**apokryphos**" and this word is from "**apo**" which is the preposition meaning "away," and "**kryptein**" which is an infinitive meaning "**to hide**." "**Crypt**" the name of an underground or hidden chamber is from "**kryptein**." Hence, "**apocrypha**" means what is hidden, doubtful, spurious, not canonical, not inspired.

Archibald Alexander founded Princeton Theological Seminary in Princeton, NJ in 1812. He was there until he died 40 years later. One of his books which I own is entitled: *The Canon Of The Old And New Testaments* and was published in 1826.

Concerning the Apocryphal books which the Catholic church has added to some Old Testaments, Archibald Alexander said the following: "After Origen, we have catalogues, in succession, not only by men of the first authority in the church, but by councils, consisting of numerous bishops, all which are perfectly the same as our own. It will be sufficient merely to refer to these sources of information. Catalogues of the books of the Old Testament have been given by Athanasius; by Cyril; by Augustine; by Jerome; by Rufin; by The Council of Laodicea, in their LX Canon: and by The Council of Carthage. And when it is considered, that all these catalogues exactly correspond with our present Canon of the Hebrew Bible, the evidence, I think, must appear complete to every impartial mind, that the Canon of the Old Testament is settled upon the clearest historical grounds. There seems to be nothing to be wished for further, in the confirmation of this point.

"But if all this testimony had been wanting, there is still a source of evidence, to which we might refer with the utmost confidence, as perfectly conclusive on this point; I mean the fact that these books have been, ever since the time of Christ and his apostles, in the keeping of both Jews and Christians, who have been constantly arrayed in opposition to each other; so that it was impossible, that any change should have been made in the Canon, by either party, without being immediately detected by the other. And the conclusive evidence that no alteration in the Canon has occurred, is, the perfect agreement of these hostile parties, in regard to the books of the Old Testament, at this time. On this point, the Jew and Christian are harmonious. There is no complaint of addition or diminution of the sacred books, on either side. The Hebrew Bible of the Jew, is the Bible of the Christian. There is here no difference. A learned Jew and Christian have even been united, in publishing an excellent edition of the Hebrew Bible. Now, if any alteration in the Canon has occurred, it must have been by the concert, or collusion of both parties, but how absurd this idea is, must be manifest to all.

"I acknowledge what is here said of the agreement of Christians and Jews, can only be said in relation to Protestant Christians. For as to those of the Romanist and Greek Communions, they have admitted other books into the Canon, which Jews and Protestants hold to be Apocryphal; but these books will form the subject of a particular discussion, in the sequel of this work." (pages 35, 36.)

"The first argument by which it may be proved that these books do not belong to the Canon of the Old Testament, is, that they are not found in the Hebrew Bible. They are not written in the Hebrew language, but in Greek, which was not known to the Jews, until long after inspiration had ceased, and the Canon of the Old Testament was closed.

"Hottinger, indeed, informs us, that he had seen the whole of the Apocrypha in pure Hebrew, among the Jews; but he entertains no doubt, that it was translated into that language, in modern times: just as the whole New Testament has recently been translated into pure Hebrew.

"It is the common opinion of the Jews, and of the Christian fathers, that Malachi was the last of the Old Testament prophets. Books written by uncertain authors, afterwards, have no claim to be reckoned Canonical; and there is good reason for believing, that those books were written long after the time of Ezra and Malachi, and some of them, perhaps, later than the commencement of the Christian era.

"These books, though probably written by Jews, have never been received into the Canon, by that people. In this, the ancient and modern Jews are of the same mind. Josephus declares, 'That no more than twenty-two books were received as inspired by his nation.' Philo who refers often to the Old Testament, in his writings, never makes the least mention of them; nor are they recognized in the Talmud, as Canonical." (pages 45, 46.)

Josephus and Philo were Jewish scholars and historians who lived when Jesus was on earth.

Archibald Alexander also said concerning the Apocryphal books, "The third argument against the Canonical authority of these books, is derived from the total silence respecting them, in the New Testament. They are never quoted by Christ and his apostles. This fact, however, is disputed by Romanists, and they even attempt to establish their right to a place in the Canon, from the citations, which they pretend have been made from these books by the apostles. They refer to Romans 11 and Hebrews 11 where they allege, that Paul has cited passages from the Book of Wisdom. 'For who hath known the mind of the Lord, or who hath been his counselor?' 'For before his translation he had this testimony that he pleased God.' But both these passages are taken directly from the Canonical books of the Old Testament. The first is nearly in the words of Isaiah; and the last from the book of Genesis; their other examples are as wide of the mark as these, and need not be set down." (pages 49, 50.)

"Origen also says, 'We should not be ignorant, that the Canonical books are the same which the Hebrews delivered unto us, and are twenty two in number, according to the number of letters of the Hebrew alphabet.' Then he sets down, in order, the names of the books, in Greek and Hebrew." (page 52.)

"Jerome, in his Epistle to Paulinus, gives us a catalogue of the books of the Old Testament, exactly corresponding with that which Protestants receive. 'Which,' says he, 'we believe agreeably to the tradition of our ancestors, to have been inspired by the Holy Spirit." (page 54.)

Some Important Observations

1. Scholars say that only one of the Apocryphal books even claims to be inspired and that it contains internal evidences which indicate it is not inspired.

2. The Apocryphal books were not written by prophets and inspired men but by writers who wrote of their labors in a way wholly incompatible with divine inspiration.

3. Jerome of the Fourth Century A.D. gave the world the Latin Vulgate translation of the Bible. This translation was acknowledged by the Roman Catholic Council which was held in Trent, Austria in 1546 to be the official Bible of the Catholic Church. The same church

added the Apocrypha to the Bible, but Jerome who made the Latin Vulgate translation explained that the Apocryphal books were not a part of the inspired canon of Scripture.

The distinguished scholar, Dr. Gleason Archer, Jr. gives many insights concerning the Apocrypha. The following is one of them. "The first argument adduced in favor of the Apocrypha is that the early versions contained them. This, however, is only partially true. Certainly the Aramaic Targums did not recognize them. Not even the Syriac Peshitta in its earliest form contained a single apocryphal book; it was only later that some of them were added. We have just seen that Jerome, the great translator of the Scriptures into Latin, did not recognize the Apocrypha as being of equal authority with the books of the Hebrew canon." (*A Survey Of Old Testament Introduction*, Moody Press, Chicago, 1994, page 81.)

4. The Apocrypha was not received as a part of God's word by the so-called "church fathers." In another book by Archibald Alexander, entitled *Alexander's Evidences of Christianity*, he says "the church fathers" or "Christian fathers" of the early centuries A.D., did not accept the Apocryphal books as part of the Sacred Old Testament Canon of Scripture. He wrote the following on this matter.

"The fourth argument against the divine authority of these books is, that they were not received as inspired by the Christian fathers; but were expressly rejected from the sacred canon, almost with one consent, by those who were best qualified to judge of their claims. In all the catalogues drawn up by fathers and councils, for the very purpose of teaching the Church what books should be received as of divine authority, these are uniformly omitted. Justin Martyr, Origen, Athanasius, Hilary, Gregory Nazianzen, Jerome, Epipanius, and Cyril, together with councils of Laodicea and Carthage, have left catalogues of the canonical books of the Old Testament, among which, not one of these is to be found. And they almost all number the books agreeably to the Jewish custom, and make the number twenty-two, according to the number of letters in the Hebrew Alphabet. And not only so, but many of these learned fathers make express mention of these books, and explicitly reject them from the sacred canon. This is especially the case in regard to Jerome, who wrote prefaces to most of the books of the Old Testament, and in these he takes occasion to mention those now in question, and declares them all to be apocryphal. And this continued to be the common opinion among the most learned theologians down to the time of the Reformation, as Dr. Cosins has abundantly shown in his *'Scholastic History of the Canon of the Old Testament.'"* (pages 261,262.)

Be sure to remember as stated in Chapter Two, the twenty-two books of the Jewish Canon of the Old Testament contain the same as the thirty-nine books of our Old Testament.

The Puritans

The Puritans disapproved of the Apocryphal books which are in the Catholic English Old Testament. They rejected these books because they were not a part of the original Hebrew text of the Old Testament.

Catholics sometimes say that they cannot study the Bible with those of other beliefs because they say their Bible is different, so they think there is no common ground from which to proceed in such study. However, the main difference between the Catholic Bible and other Bibles is that in the Catholic Bible there are the fourteen apocryphal books. But these fourteen books do not teach the doctrines of the Catholic Church. So, these books are not any help to Catholics in their efforts to justify their beliefs and practices.

Neither the Catholic Bible, nor any other Bible teaches people to be Catholics or Protestants. The Catholic Bible like any other Bible teaches people just to be Christians. The Catholic Bible like any other Bible teaches all people to be one in Christ and all to be members of the one church about which we read in any Bible. (John 17; Colossians 1:18; Ephesians 1:22,23.) The Catholic Bible, like any other Bible teaches people how to be baptized into Christ to reach the saving power of his precious blood which is the same as being baptized into the body of Christ which is his church.

The Catholic Bible, like any other Bible teaches all people how to be brothers and sisters in Christ and his church and love and esteem each other.

Do not let the uninspired books known as the Apocryphal books keep you from knowing the truth about the Bible.

Questions And Discussion Points

1. What does apocryphal mean?

2. Who was Archibald Alexander?

3. Discuss the quotations in the lesson from Archibald Alexander.

4. Do the Apocryphal books claim to be inspired? Discuss.

5. Discuss Jerome and his translation and what he said about the Apocryphal books.

6. What did the Puritans think about the Apocryphal books?

7. Do the Apocryphal books teach the doctrines of the Catholic church? Discuss.

8. What will one be if he follows the Catholic Bible?

Chapter Six

THE "DOCUMENTARY HYPOTHESIS"
AND THE OLD TESTAMENT

Scholars say that before the end of the 17th Century A.D. the trustworthiness of the Bible was doubted relatively little. Beginning in the 18th Century some who came to be called "higher critics" who were motivated by false philosophy, began to launch attacks on the Bible. They asserted that their philosophy was sovereign over religion. This caused some exegetes or interpreters of the Bible to exert great endeavors to try to explain away all miracles of the Bible and interpret theology in light of their false philosophy and subjective and wishful thinking. For an example, Remarus said the story of Christ's resurrection was based on a fraudulent scheme of His disciples. F. V. Reinhard and others said Jesus was merely a teacher of morality. That was inconsistent because the New Testament is the source that declares Jesus taught morality. It also says Jesus claimed to have come into this world from the Father in heaven, and that He was God's Son. If He was not what He said He was, He was a liar, and therefore not even a good person!

The age of so-called critical scholarship seems to have been born in Germany and spread to other countries, especially England and America.

Eventually some "scholars" rejected the Bible as a reliable source, and what was in it that did not agree with "scholarly" standards of authenticity should be rejected.

The history of the "higher criticism" movement is much too complex and massive even to summarize adequately in this chapter. There are many classic works on this history.

Eventually the "higher critics" denied that Moses wrote the first five books of the Old Testament called the Pentateuch but were written instead by various authors hundreds of years after Moses' time.

One of the textbooks that I used while a student at Eastern Kentucky State College (now University) is entitled: *Our Heritage Of World Literature*. In a chapter on the Bible, the authors say that the first five books of the Old Testament were welded together out of ninth and eighth century B.C. materials in the fourth century B.C. This concept of the authorship of the Pentateuch, or the first five books of the Old Testament, is part of a view regarding the authorship of the Old Testament known as the "documentary hypothesis" or the "fragmentary hypothesis," or the "JEPD hypothesis." These critics say that the Pentateuch is the product of various writers who lived many hundreds of years after Moses is supposed to have lived.

It is affirmed that fragments of writings were compiled by various editors into what we call the Pentateuch. The fragments are supposed to have been written by various writers. Similar ideas are presented in the hypothesis concerning the explanation of the rest of the Old Testament. The exponents of this explanation of the origin of the Old Testament said that Moses, even if there was such a man, could not have written the Pentateuch about 1500 B.C., because, they said writing was not done that early. They said it was written instead hundreds of years later by unknown writers known by certain classifications. These classifications are abbreviated with the letters J, E, P, and D. These stand for the names of certain classifications of writers.

Actually, J, E, P, and D, and their documents have never been discovered; they only exist in the minds of naturalistic theologians who needed some way to fit the Old Testament into the doctrine of evolutionary history they already accepted before they ever conceived of such a scheme by which to account for the Old Testament's origin.

The fragmentary hypothesis is thought by some misled souls to be a scholarly approach to the origin of the Old Testament. However, the truth is that the hypothesis is not scholarly at all.

Some say the so-called "higher critics" first attacked the Book of Deuteronomy. When Jesus endured the series of temptations of the archfiend of mankind, according to Matthew chapter four and Luke chapter four, in response to each of the temptations, our Lord quoted Holy Scripture. Each time He quoted from Deuteronomy.

Approximately eighteen centuries after Jesus did this, the "higher critics" who were agents of Satan, attacked the Old Testament in evil attempts to prove it was not written by men who were inspired of God. They first attacked the Book of Deuteronomy! Maybe this all means that time means nothing to Satan. Eighteen hundred years after Jesus overcame his temptations by quoting three times from Deuteronomy, Satan was fighting back through the "higher critics!

I have a copy of *The Authorship of Deuteronomy* by J. W. McGarvey, which was published in 1902 by the Standard Publishing Company of Cincinnati, OH. In this classic book brother McGarvey refuted the false charges and assertions that so-called "higher critics" made against the Book of Deuteronomy. J. W. McGarvey's body lies in Lexington Cemetery in Lexington, KY. He lived in Lexington for 49 years. One of the houses in which he lived stands in Lexington. When my family and I lived in Lexington I knew people who knew brother McGarvey. He died in 1911, but "he being dead yet speaketh" in his many good books!

There are many classical works which defend the Bible, and which present the evidences that it was written by inspired writers. Many of these great classical works deal with the authorship of the Pentateuch.

Anyone who believes the fragmentary hypothesis surely could see the folly of that hypothesis by reading such works as: *The Authorship Of Deuteronomy*, by J. W. McGarvey; *An Introduction To The Old Testament*, by Dr. Edward Young; *The Pentateuch, Its Origin And Structure*, by Edwin Cone Bissell; *The Mosaic Origin Of The Pentateuchal Codes*, by Gerhardus Vos; *Moses And The Prophets*, by William Henry Green; *The Problems Of The Old Testament*, by James Orr; and *The Five Books Of Moses*, by Osward T. Allis. These are just a few of the host of classical works in this field of study.

When my family and I lived in Lexington, KY (1960-1968), one of the Christian students who attended the University of Kentucky, and who attended the church where I preached told me he was quite disturbed by what some professors at the university had said in teaching the documentary hypothesis about the origin of the Old Testament. I lent him some of the books listed in the foregoing paragraph and insisted that he read them. Several days later he told me he had read them and he was very pleased with the way the authors of the books refuted what his professors had said. Then he said, "I cannot understand how my professors can believe what they believe on that subject!"

I could understand why! They were ignorant of the arguments that refute the documentary hypothesis about the Old Testament! I had taken a course at the University of Kentucky in my Master's degree program, on the History of the Jews which was taught by a Jew and he taught the documentary hypothesis. When I asked him in class if he had read any of the books listed above, he said he had never heard of any of them or any of the authors! I was told before taking that class that its teacher who had a Ph.D. was one of the greatest authorities in the United States on the Old Testament! No one should be called a scholar who knows nothing about what refutes the views which he thinks are valid!

Discoveries That Refute Claims

Some have objected to the Mosaic authorship of the first five books of the Old Testament on the assumption that writing was unknown and not practiced at the time that Moses lived, about 1500 B.C. Several discoveries have made this objection invalid. Archaeological discoveries have proven that writing was a science not only around 1500 B.C., but hundreds of years before that.

In 1929 the Ras Shamra texts were discovered. These are conceded to have been written in the 15th and early 14th centuries before Christ. These texts prove that writing was practiced by the Canaanites by the middle of the second millennium before Christ. (Edward J. Young, *An Introduction To The Old Testament*, page 62)

In 1935 there were discovered at a place called Mari in the Euphrates River Valley over 20,000 tablets, most of which belong to the early part of the second millennium before Christ. This proved that writing was practiced hundreds of years before Moses lived. These Mari tablets confirm the biblical account that Israel's ancestors went to Palestine by way of the region of Haran. (Edward J. Young, Ibid.)

Many other confirmations of the accuracy of Bible history are given in these Mari tablets, and other unearthed instruments. Two critics, Wellhausen and Graf advanced the view that Moses could not have written the first five books of the Old Testament because writing was not practiced when Moses lived. Their claim was exploded by the spade!

Others have argued that Moses could not have written the first five books of the Old Testament, the Pentateuch, because there are words in those books that were not used in 1500 B.C. But scholars have proven that the words which some say were not in use in about 1500 B.C., were indeed used in 1500 B.C., and even hundreds of years before that time!

Others say that moral and social laws of the Pentateuch reflect a moral and social level too high for the times referred to in the Pentateuch. This objection is based on the abominable assumption that man gradually developed his morality without any help from a beneficent Creator.

God revealed moral principles to man before he gave the Law to Moses. God instructed man how to live right from the very beginning when Adam and Eve were created by him. Man did not always live by the standard of right that God gave to him, but the Old Testament, even the Pentateuch does reflect a high level of moral and social status. That is true because God revealed such a high level, even though the ones to whom he revealed it did not always live by it!

Scholars say that archaeological discoveries reveal the same high level of living for the times referred to in the Pentateuch that it presents. Again, we insist that the spade of the scholar has confirmed the pages of the inspired scribes!

The Prophet Daniel And The Book That Bears His Name

"In fact, it is the testimony of both Jewish and Christian tradition that Daniel, living at the royal court in Babylon, composed his book during the sixth century B.C. That this traditional thesis is correct may be seen from the following considerations." (Edward J. Young, Th. M., Ph.D., *An Introduction To The Old Testament*, page 351.) Dr. Young then presents nine or more valid reasons for saying Daniel wrote his book in the 500's B.C. One of these reasons is that Jesus Christ quoted Daniel in Matthew 24:15. (See Daniel 9:27; 12:11.) Christ expressed no doubt about Daniel's authorship of the Book of Daniel. He did not say, "Be at Central Synagogue next Tuesday at 7:00 p.m. when I will lecture on the proofs that what I said Daniel the prophet said was really and truly said by him, and that he really did write the Book of Daniel." There is no evidence that the Jews of Jesus time on earth had any doubts about this matter!

Porphyry was a neo-Platonic philosopher who lived in the third century A.D. He denied that Daniel wrote the Book of Daniel. He said the author was someone who lived in the time of Antiochus Epiphanes who died in 92 B.C. Porphyry and other negative critics of the Bible have said the Book of Daniel speaks so accurately about the history of kingdoms that it had to be written as history, after the facts, and that it could not have been written by Daniel or anyone else before the history occurred. They could not prove that charge. The only reason they made that charge was because they did not believe Daniel or anyone else could have prophesied so accurately great events and the rising and falling of several kingdoms during several centuries. They did not believe Daniel was inspired of God! Those who do not believe he was, think accurate predictive prophecy is impossible. That unbelief does not prove that Daniel was not inspired of God, or that any writer of the Old Testament was not guided by the Holy Ghost in what he wrote.

The Jewish historian, Flavius Josephus, who was contemporary with Jesus of Nazareth, wrote about Alexander the Great who died in 320 B.C. Josephus says Alexander entered Jerusalem with his army. He wrote of Alexander's entry into that great Jewish city as follows. "And when he went up into the temple, he offered sacrifice to God, according to the high priest's direction, and magnificently treated both the high priest and the priests. And when the book of Daniel was showed him, wherein Daniel declared that one of the Greeks should destroy the empire of the Persians, he supposed that himself was the person intended; and as he was then glad, he dismissed the multitude for the present, but the next day he called them to him, and bade them ask what favours they pleased of him; whereupon the high priest desired that they might enjoy the laws of their forefathers, and might pay no tribute on the seventh year. He granted all they desired." (*The Works Of Flavius Josephus*, page 350.)

Alexander was right! Daniel did refer to him in his God given interpretation of Nebuchadnezzar's dream. (Daniel 2.) Evidently, he also referred to him in Daniel 7:6; 8:3-8, 20-22; and 11:3.

According to Josephus, Alexander the Great read from the Book of Daniel, before 320 B.C. which was at least 150 to 200 years before that book was written according to some "intellectuals" who are called "higher critics" of the Bible. One of their main difficulties is that they bit into a Critic that is as much higher than they are as the heavens are higher than the earth! That higher Critic is the word of God! "For the word of God is living and powerful, and sharper than any two-edged sword, piercing even to the division of soul and spirit, and of joints and marrow, and is a discerner of the thoughts and intents of the heart." (Hebrews 4:12.) The word "discerner" in this text is the translation of the Greek word "**kritikos**," and our word "critic" is an Anglicized form of that word!

The word of God is indeed the highest of all critics. God said to Israel, "For My thoughts are not your thoughts, nor are your ways My ways, says the Lord. For as the heavens are higher than the earth, so are My ways higher than your ways, and My thoughts than your thoughts." (Isaiah 55:8,9.)

Questions And Discussion Points

If Jesus did not come from the Father in heaven as He said he did, was He a good man? Why?

Let someone tell what the "documentary hypothesis" is.

What is the story in the lesson about a University of Kentucky professor?

What are the Ras Shamra texts?

What were discovered in Mari in the Euphrates River Valley in 1935?

Did God reveal moral principles to mankind before He gave the Law of Moses? Discuss.

Who was Porphyry?

What book was shown to Alexander the Great in Jerusalem? Discuss.

Chapter Seven

THE DEAD SEA SCROLLS

The Dead Sea Scrolls After Forty Years is the title of a book copyrighted in 1991 by the Biblical Archaeology Society, 3000 Connecticut Avenue, N.W. in Washington D.C. It is composed of lectures made at a Symposium at the Smithsonian Institution October 27, 1990. These lectures were made by four of the world's most distinguished scholars on the Dead Sea Scrolls. They are as follows.

1. Dr. Hershel Shanks is founder, editor, and publisher of *Biblical Archaeology And Review and Bible Review*. He is a prolific writer. He is a graduate of Harvard Law School and has published many treatises on legal topics.

2. Dr. P. Kyle McCarter, Jr. is the William Foxwell Albright Professor of Biblical and Ancient Near Eastern Studies at Johns Hopkins University in Baltimore, Maryland. He taught 11 years at the University of Virginia. He is the author of several books, including commentaries on the Old Testament books of First and Second Samuel.

3. Dr. James C. Vanderkam is a professor of religion at North Carolina State University. He has written extensively on biblical languages and literature for many prominent publications.

4. Dr. James A. Sanders is a professor of intertestamental and biblical studies at the School of Theology at Claremont, California, and professor of religion in the Claremont Graduate School. He is founder and president of the Ancient Biblical Manuscript Center for Preservation and Research, where he has developed an archive of thousands of biblical manuscripts on negatives, including all the Dead Sea Scrolls.

I have listed the names of these four men and some of their high qualifications and signal accomplishments to show that they are not novices and amateurs. I have gleaned from their lectures most of the information that follows.

The Discovery Of The Dead Sea Scrolls

Not far from where a young shepherd boy named David threw a stone with a sling that killed a giant named Goliath, about 3000 years later in 1947 a young shepherd boy named Muhammad Adah-Dhib threw a stone into a cave that caused the discovery of some now very famous and important manuscripts named the Dead Sea Scrolls.

Along the northwestern shore of the Dead Sea on a plain between that lifeless sea and some of the caves where the scrolls were found are the ruins of an ancient city called Khirbet Qumran. Scholars think it was begun between 700 and 800 years before Christ was born. The ruins include a large cistern and some walls.

Muhammad Adah-Dhib was one of a group of the Ta'Amireh tribe who were Bedouin shepherds searching for some of their sheep near the northwest corner of the Dead Sea in an area where there were numerous caves. Muhammad cast a stone into the caves and heard "a crashing sound" when the stone crushed a pottery vessel.

The next day a group of the Ta'Amireh went into the cave and found some scrolls, and they did not know what they were. They took their find to Bethelehem. Eventually, the scrolls were in the custody of a man named Kando who died about 1989.

These scrolls were found the year before the United Nations Council declared the formation of the State of Israel in 1948.

The famous scholar William Foxwell Albright saw one of the fragments of the scrolls and recognized it as genuine and about 2000 years old.

There were seven scrolls in Cave I. One of them is a scroll of Isaiah about 1000 years older then the next oldest text of Isaiah which is one of what are known as the Masoret Texts of the Old Testament. I had a course in Hebrew at Lexington Theological Seminary in Lexington, Kentucky. Dr. William Reed, the teacher, showed us a copy of Isaiah Chapter Six from the Dead Sea Scroll text of Isaiah and we students read it. Dr. Reed commented that the one who wrote it in Hebrew was not good at handwriting!

For several years Bedouin and Professional Archaeologists found scrolls in ten more caves in the Qumrun area. The biggest find was over 500 scrolls in Cave IV. Most of these are in fragments and mixed up and had to be separated and organized. An international team under the auspices of the Jordanian Government worked until 1960 before they got the fragments arranged between glass. As of 1991, 80% of these remained unpublished.

The seven scrolls of Cave I were promptly published by American and Israeli scholars.

There are some variations in the reports regarding the number of scrolls found in the eleven caves. Some say the total is 800. *Dead Sea Scrolls – A New Translation – Translated And With Commentary* is the title of a book by Michael Wise, Martin Abegg, Jr., and Edward Cook, which was published in 1996 by Harper San Francisco. They give a good insight on the scrolls in the following excerpt on page 5.

"When people use the phrase 'Dead Sea Scrolls,' they sometimes mean all of these treasure troves, but more usually only the Qumran scrolls are meant. That will be our own usage in the pages that follow.

"The total number of scrolls, when the books were intact, may have been as high as 1,000. Some have vanished without a trace, but scholars have identified the remains of about 870 separate scrolls. Their long centuries in the earth have reduced the vast majority of them to bits and pieces, mere scraps, some no larger than a fingernail. The fourth cave alone, where the biggest cache of manuscripts was unearthed, contained an estimated 15,000 fragments."

Archaeologists Uncover Ancient Graves Near Site Where Dead Sea Scrolls Found is the title of an Associated Press news story by Steve Weizmar in the July 27, 2001 edition of the *Times Daily* in Florence, AL. He says, "The first of the Dead Sea Scrolls was discovered in 1947 by Bedouin shepherds pursuing a lost animal. A total of 900 volumes have been recovered since."

Classifications Of The Scrolls

The documents called the Dead Sea Scrolls are classified as follows.

1. The biblical texts. The Jews say there are 22 books in the Old Testament. These 22 books contain exactly the same writings that we call the 39 books of the Old Testament. When it is said, as many say, that the Dead Sea Scrolls contain all, or parts of all of the Old Testament books except Esther, that needs to be clarified. Some others of the 39 books nor portions of them are not in the Dead Sea Scrolls. According to the Hebrew count of 22 books in the Old Testament Canon, all of the 22 books either whole or in part are in the Dead Sea Scrolls except Esther. For examples, the Hebrew-Canon contains First and Second Samuel as one book; and First and Second Kings as one book; and First and Second Chronicles as one book, etc.

On page 27 of the book cited above, Dr. James Vanderkam says Ezra and Nehemiah are one book in the Hebrew Canon, and that some of Ezra is in the Dead Sea Scrolls, but none of Nehemiah. He also says there are some such cases in the Minor Prophets, which in the Hebrew Canon are one book. He says, "The Book Of The Twelve Prophets is attested but not all its parts."

2. The second category of Dead Sea Scrolls is classified as The Apocryphal and The Pseudepigraphous writings. Apocryphal means not canonical or not inspired. Pseudepigraphous is the adjective that describes documents written under others' names.

3. The Sectarian Scrolls. There is controversy concerning who wrote these. Some think a Jewish sect called the Essenes wrote them. Others think the Qumran sect wrote them. These scrolls include (1) The War Scrolls; (2) The Damascus Document; and (3) The Manual of Discipline or Community Rule.

4. There is a mixture of manuscripts in Hebrew, Greek, and Aramaic. Most of these are leather scrolls. One is a copper scroll.

5. The fifth category is a 28 feet long document called The Temple Scroll.

Many believe the Dead Sea Scrolls were taken to the caves from Jerusalem.

Numbers Of Old Testament Books In The Dead Sea Scrolls

Reclaiming The Dead Sea Scrolls is the name of a book written by Lawrence H. Schiffman and published by Doubleday Company in 1995. In this book on page 163, Dr. Schiffman lists the number of Old Testament books he says are represented in the Dead Sea Scrolls as follows: 18 of Genesis; 18 of Exodus; 17 of Leviticus; 12 of Numbers; 31 of Deuteronomy; 2 of Joshua; 3 of Judges; 4 of 1 and 2 Samuel; 3 of 1 and 2 Kings; 22 of Isaiah; 6 of Jeremiah; 7 of Ezekiel; 10 of the Minor Prophets; 39 of the Book of Psalms; 2 of the Book of Proverbs; 4 of Job; 4 of Song of Solomon; 4 of Ruth; 4 of Lamentations; 2 of Ecclesiastes; 8 of Daniel; 1 of Ezra and Nehemiah; and 1 of 1 and 2 Chronicles.

Writings Other Than Old Testament Books

Wise, Abegg, and Cook, in their book already cited, make a very good point about how profoundly the Old Testament Scriptures influenced the most of the other writings found in the Dead Sea Scrolls. Almost all of these scrolls that are not copies of Old Testament books are connected in one way or another with the Old Testament Scriptures. The poetic compositions are filled with Old Testament phrases. The legal texts are based on Old Testament teachings. The narratives of past matters and predictions regarding the future are repetitions of Old Testament stories or Old Testament prophecies.

Doctors Wise, Abegg, and Cook tell about a commentary on the Old Testament Book of Habakkuk that is one of the Dead Sea Scrolls found in Cave I. They say it has been the subject of several commentaries. The following are other interesting and informative matters presented by these three scholars.

Five commentaries on Isaiah were found in Cave IV. Ten fragments of one of these have been reconstructed into three columns of text of Isaiah and commentary.

A commentary on the Old Testament Book of Nahum found in one of the Qumran caves may be the most important scroll of all for determining the history behind the Dead Sea Scrolls. The author gives a number of reasons why.

Dr. James Vanderkam says six commentaries on Isaiah are in the Dead Sea Scrolls. He also says there are 2 on Micah; 2 on Zephaniah; 4 on some of the Psalms; 2 on Hosea; and 1 on Nahum. Some of these are comments on whole books and some on selected passages from several books.

Wise, Abegg, and Cook say there are two Aramaic translations of the Book of Job in the Dead Sea Scrolls, and they think that book was translated into Aramaic because they say, "The Hebrew of Job is unquestionably the most difficult of the Old Testament."

These three scholars comment on A Sermon On The Flood in the Dead Sea Scrolls. The text used in the sermon is Genesis chapters six through nine. The first part of the sermon is a description of the great flood. The second part is the application and admonition. Who the preacher was is not mentioned, nor the audience to whom the sermon was preached. One of the main points of the sermon is that the sheer abundance of God's creation had a corrupting influence. The idea must have been that people are so blessed by God that they take his abundant gifts for granted and become ungrateful. Paul wrote about this in Romans 1:21 which says, "Because that, when they knew God, they glorified him not as God, neither were thankful; but became vain in their imaginations, and their foolish heart was darkened."

Some Of The Other Subjects

Wise, Abegg, and Cook present a list of 131 subjects of lessons in the Dead Sea Scrolls most of which are related to the Old Testament

Scriptures. Eighteen of these are: (1) Tales of the Patriarchs; (2) The Words of Moses; (3) A List Of Buried Treasure – The Copper Scroll; (4) A Collection of Messianic Proof Texts; (5) A Commentary on Consoling Passages in Old Testament Scripture; (6) The Last Words of Naphtali; (7) The Vision of Daniel; (8) A Commentary on the Law of Moses; (9) Commentaries on Genesis; (10) Laws About Gleanings; (11) The Sabbaths and Festivals of the Year; (12) God the Creator; (13) In Praise of God's Grace; (14) Hymns of Thanksgiving; (15) Lives of the Patriarchs; (16) A Record of Discipling Action; (17) Daily Prayers; and (18) A Biblical Chronology.

Languages Of The Dead Sea Scrolls

Dr. John J. Collins, professor of Old Testament at Yale University, and Dr. Robert A. Kugler of Gonzaga University in Spokane, Washington are the editors of a book entitled: *Religion In The Dead Sea Scrolls*. One contributor to this book is Dr. Timothy H. Lim of the Department of Hebrew and Old Testament at the University of Edinburgh. In the book under the heading, Languages Of Qumran Scrolls: Hebrew, Aramaic, Greek, Dr. Lim says 90 percent of the Dead Sea Scrolls are in Hebrew; seven percent are in Aramaic; and three percent are in Greek. He thinks the Qumran Library (Dead Sea Scrolls) are on the religious beliefs of the Qumran community and also the beliefs of Second Temple Judaism. On page 58, after commenting on the Hebrew and Aramaic documents of the Dead Sea Scrolls, Dr. Lim says, "What I have begun to do is investigate the multilingual context of the Qumran community by examining the other language attested among the Qumran scrolls, namely, Greek. Did the Qumran community know Greek? If so, how much Greek did they know? Were they able to converse fluently in it? Could they write a literary composition, or is their written language largely functional – writing short missives and notes? Were they fluent enough in both languages to be able to translate a text from Hebrew into Greek?"

Conclusion

From all in this chapter it is easy to conclude that the Qumran people were great students of the Old Testament Scriptures.

It is also easy to detect that there is considerable interest in the Dead Sea Scrolls. Dr. Hershel Shanks says, "A scholar in Kansas has assembled over 10,000 articles that have been written about the Dead Sea Scrolls." (*The Dead Sea Scrolls After Forty Years*, page 13.)

The site of the ruins of ancient Khirbet Qumran is on an elevated and blighted terrace where nothing grows, and nothing moves among the quiet stones. The strange blue Dead Sea is well seen from the ruins of the ancient city. The wafting, sighing, whispering winds blow through the rocks and rubble and ruins where ancient people obviously sought earnestly after God. The record they left in their library in their caves gives us a clearer perception of the religious climate into which the Good Shepherd was born of the virgin Mary in a barn in Bethlehem where "the word became flesh and dwelt among us" not far from Khirbet Qumran!

Questions And Discussion Points

What is said in the lesson about David and Muhammad Adah-Dhib?

What was the Ta'Amireh?

How many scrolls were found in Cave I?

What are the five classifications of the Dead Sea Scrolls?

Are there copies of all 39 books of the Old Testament in the scrolls?

How many commentaries on Isaiah are in the scrolls?

What three languages are in the scrolls?

How many articles about the scrolls has a Kansas scholar collected according to Dr. Shanks?

Chapter Eight

THE LAW OF MOSES INCLUDED THE TEN COMMANDMENTS

"And God spake all these words, saying, I am the Lord thy God, which have brought thee out of the land of Egypt, out of the house of bondage.

1. "Thou shalt have no other gods before me.

2. "Thou shalt not make unto thee any graven image, or any likeness of any thing that is in heaven above, or that is in the earth beneath, or that is in the water under the earth: thou shalt not bow down thyself to them, nor serve them, for I the Lord thy God am a jealous God, visiting the iniquity of the fathers upon the children unto the third and fourth generation of them that hate me: and shewing mercy unto thousands of them that love me, and keep my commandments.

3. "Thou shalt not take the name of the Lord thy God in vain; for the Lord will not hold him guiltless that taketh his name in vain.

4. "Remember the sabbath day, to keep it holy. Six days shalt thou labour, and do all thy work: but the seventh day is the sabbath of the Lord thy God: in it thou shalt not do any work, thou, nor thy son, nor thy daughter, thy manservant, nor thy maidservant, nor thy cattle, nor thy stranger that is within thy gates: for in six days the Lord made heaven and earth, the sea and all that in them is, and rested the seventh day: wherefore the Lord blessed the sabbath day and hallowed it.

5. "Honour thy father and thy mother: that thy days may be long upon the land which the Lord thy God giveth thee.

6. "Thou shalt not kill.

7. "Thou shalt not commit adultery.

8. "Thou shalt not steal.

9. "Thou shalt not bear false witness against thy neighbor.

10. "Thou shalt not covet thy neighbor's house, thou shalt not covet thy neighbor's wife, nor his manservant, nor his maidservant, nor his ox, nor his ass, nor anything that is thy neighbor's." (Exodus 20:1-17.)

God gave the foregoing ten commandments to Moses on Mount Sinai. The ones that are moral laws are not a complete moral code.

They did not deal with every specific form of sin and immorality. For an example, number seven does not specify every form of sexual impurity. Number nine does not explicitly forbid all kinds of lying. It does not specify not lying to one's neighbor, but only forbids bearing false witness against one's neighbor. It forbids lying about one's neighbor but does not forbid lying to one's neighbor. This does not mean that such conduct not specified in the ten commandments was not forbidden in the Old Testament. There are scores of other commands which God gave through Moses regarding many situations and circumstances regarding morality, worship, ceremonies and rituals in Exodus, Leviticus, Numbers, and Deuteronomy.

The name Deuteronomy was derived from **deuteros** that means second, and **nomos** that means law. So Deuteronomy means second law. Strictly, it is not a second law, but in this book Moses reminded Israel of the Law God had given them. Moses challenged Israel concerning the statutes and judgments which God had given them and charged them "Ye shall not add unto the word which I command you, neither shall you diminish aught from it that you keep the commandments of the Lord your God which I command you." (Deuteronomy 4:2.)

In Deuteronomy chapter five, Moses reminded the Israelites of the ten commandments and presented them again.

Also, it is evident that long before God gave the ten commandments on Mount Sinai, he gave laws concerning worship and morality. These laws were given through the fathers or heads of families, the patriarchs, in what we sometimes call the Patriarchal Age. These laws and standards are evident in the story of Cain and Abel, and in the fact that before the great flood of Noah's time, "God saw that the wickedness of man was great in the earth, and that every imagination of the thoughts of his heart was only evil continually." (Genesis 6:5.) Wickedness and evil were rampant because the people were violating God's laws concerning morality.

The story of Lot and his family in Sodom also shows that God had given laws of morality. The homosexuals of Sodom were violators of God's law of morality long before Moses. When they wanted the men (actually two angels) who were guests in Lot's house "that we may know them," Lot said to them, "I pray thee, do not so wickedly." (Genesis 19:7.) What they wanted to do to Lot's guests was wickedness because such was violation of God's law concerning such heinous conduct!

When Potiphar's wife tried to seduce Joseph, he asked, "How can I do this great wickedness and sin against God?" (Genesis 39:9.) It is implied that Joseph knew that such sexual conduct between those who were not married to each other was a violation of God's law!

Were The Ten Commandments Abolished When Jesus Died?

Jesus our Savior lived perfectly by the law of Moses. He taught others to live by it. "Then spake Jesus to the multitude, and to his disciples, saying, the scribes and Pharisees sit in Moses' seat: all therefore whatsoever they bid you observe, that observe and do; but do not ye after their works: for they say and do not." (Matthew 23:1-3.) When Jesus died on the cross did He abolish the very law by which He had lived and by which He had taught others to live? The right answer to this question is, yes.

Some attempt to prove that the answer to the above question is, no, by reciting the following which Jesus said. "Think not that I am come to destroy the law, or the prophets: I am not come to destroy, but to fulfill. Verily I say unto you, Till heaven and earth pass, one jot or one tittle shall in no wise pass from the law, till all be fulfilled." (Matthew 5:17,18.)

"One jot or one tittle" refers to markings in the Hebrew text of the law with which the people were familiar, and would be comparable to our saying of an English text, "the dotting of an i or the crossing of a t." Certainly Jesus was emphasizing that the law, not even a minute part of it would be destroyed or taken away till all be fulfilled. "Till all be fulfilled" is the key to the proper understanding of what Jesus said.

Jesus said He came to fulfill the law. Did He do what He came to do? Certainly He did! Therefore He fulfilled the law. He said the law would not be destroyed till all was fulfilled. But all was fulfilled, if Jesus did what He came to do. Therefore, the law was destroyed or abolished! The New Testament teaches this abundantly in many other texts. Does this mean that the ten commandments were abolished? The right answer to this question is, yes. However we are under a new law or covenant which is the law of Christ and it contains all the ten commandments that were in the law of Moses except the command to keep the seventh day sabbath. It also contains commandments which were not in the law of Moses.

There are laws in the current Constitution of the State of Alabama which were in the Constitutions of Alabama which preceded the current Constitution, but we live by these laws because they are in the current Constitution. There are also laws in the current Alabama Constitution which were not in the Constitutions which preceded it. So it is with the gospel. There are laws regarding moral conduct in the gospel which were in the law of Moses, but we follow them because they are in the new covenant which was sealed with the blood of the Son of God. The following are the ten commandments given by God through Moses and some of the references where all of them are taught in the New Testament except number four.

1. Thou shalt have no other gods before me. (1 Corinthians 8:5,6.)

2. Thou shalt not make unto thee any graven image. (1 John 5:21; Romans 2:22.)

3. Thou shalt not take the name of the Lord thy God in vain. (James 5:12; Ephesians 4:29.)

4. Remember the Sabbath day to keep it holy. This is not taught in the New Testament. Christians are taught to worship on Sunday, the first day of the week. (Acts 20:7; 1 Corinthians 16:1,2.)

5. Honour thy father and thy mother. (Ephesians 6:1,2.)

6. Thou shalt not kill. (Romans 13:9.)

7. Thou shalt not commit adultery. (Matthew 5:27,28; Romans 2:22; 13:9.)

8. Thou shalt not steal. (Ephesians 4:28; Romans 2:22.)

9. Thou shalt not bear false witness against thy neighbor. (Revelation 21:8; Ephesians 5:25.)

10. Thou shalt not covet. (Colossians 3:5; Luke 12:15.)

The main purpose of the Epistle to the Hebrews in the New Testament was to show the difference in the law of Moses and the gospel of Christ, or the difference in the old covenant under Moses and the new covenant under Christ. One of the plain passages in Hebrews on this is the following.

"Then said I, Lo, I come (in the volume of the book it is written of me) to do thy will, O God. Above when He said, Sacrifice and offering and burnt offerings and offerings for sin thou wouldest not; neither hadst pleasure therein; which are offered by the law; then said He, Lo, I come to do thy will, O God. He taketh away the first, that He may establish the second. By the which will we are sanctified through the offering of the body of Jesus Christ once for all. (Hebrews 10:7-10.)

In the context of Hebrews, "He taketh away the first" obviously refers to the law of Moses. In Hebrews chapters 8 and 10 the holy writer quoted a prophecy from Jeremiah concerning the doing away of the old law or covenant and the giving of the new covenant. Often in Hebrews the old law or testament of Moses is contrasted with the new testament or will or covenant of Christ, and it is plainly declared that the old was taken away and the new was established.

In Galatians, the apostle Paul did the same as the writer of Hebrews did. Referring to the law of Moses, Paul wrote, "Wherefore the law was our schoolmaster to bring us to Christ; that we might be justified by faith. But after that faith is come, we are no longer under a schoolmaster." (Galatians 3:24,25.) In the Greek text the article precedes faith in verse 25, and it literally means "after the faith came." All this means that after the faith or the gospel, or the new covenant came, the Jews who had been under the law of Moses, the schoolmaster, were no longer under it. That is because the law of Moses was abolished when Jesus died!

"For he is our peace, who hath made both one, and hath broken down the middle wall of partition between us; having abolished in his flesh the enmity, even the law of commandments contained in ordinances; for to make in himself of twain one new man, so making peace; and that he might reconcile both unto God in one body by the cross, having slain the enmity thereby...." (Ephesians 2:14-16.) In this Paul says the law that separated Jews and Gentiles was abolished when Jesus died, and both Jews and Gentiles are reconciled unto God in the one body which is the church. He says all this was done by the cross, meaning, obviously, by the death of Jesus on the cross.

In Colossians 2:14 Paul said this same thing when he said that Jesus blotted out the handwriting of ordinances and took it out of the way nailing it to his cross.

New High Priest "After The Law"

The Book of Hebrews also clearly shows that the order of high priests under the law of Moses was superceded by the high priesthood of Jesus Christ after the law of Moses was abolished. The following is one of the statements in Hebrews that makes this cardinal truth plain.

"And inasmuch as He was not made priest without an oath (for they have become priests without an oath, but He with an oath by Him who said to Him: 'The Lord has sworn and will not relent, "You are a priest forever according to the order of Melchizedek"'), by so much more Jesus has become a surety of a better covenant. And there were many priests, because they were prevented by death from continuing. But He, because He continues forever, has an unchangeable priesthood. Therefore He is also able to save to the uttermost those who come to God through Him, since He ever lives to make intercession for them. For such a High Priest was fitting for us, who is holy, harmless, undefiled, separate from sinners, and has become higher than the heavens; who does not need daily, as those high priests, to offer up sacrifices, first for His own sins and then for the people's, for this He did once for all when He offered up Himself. For the law appoints as high priests men who have weakness, but the word of the oath, which came after the law, appoints the Son who has been perfected forever." (Hebrews 7:20-28.)

Verse 28 clearly affirms that our Lord Jesus became High Priest "after the law." "The law" obviously refers to the law of Moses, and the text means that law was abolished.

Questions And Discussion Points

Are the moral laws of the ten commandments a complete moral code? Discuss.

What does "Deuteronomy" mean?

What are some examples in the book of Genesis that make it evident that God gave moral laws before he gave the ten commandments to Moses?

What did Jesus mean by "one jot or one tittle"?

How many of the Mosaic ten commandments are in the New Testament?

Discuss Ephesians 2:14-16 and Colossians 2:14 and compare them.

Read and discuss Hebrews 7:20-28.

Did Jesus become High Priest over God's house the church before he abolished that law?

Chapter Nine

MORE IN THE OLD TESTAMENT
THAN THE LAW OF MOSES

The Old Testament and the New Testament constitute the two major parts or sections of the Bible. They are both the word of God in the sense that God directed the approximately 40 writers who wrote them, by the process of Divine Inspiration!

We must not equate the Old Testament and the Law of Moses. That law is in the Old Testament, but there are also many other matters of history and unchanging principles of life in the Old Testament. In another chapter I present some of the abundance of evidence in the Bible that when Jesus Christ of Nazareth, the Son of God, died on a Roman cross, He thereby abolished the law of Moses, but this does not mean we do not still have the book called the Old Testament in which we can read the stories of patriarchs, prophets, potentates, priests, and poets, and learn from examples in those stories of faith in, and obedience to God. We can also learn how unfaithfulness to God, and evil ways are not the way to live.

After quoting from the Old Testament, the apostle Paul wrote, "For whatever things were written before were written for our learning, that we through the patience and comfort of the Scriptures might have hope." (Romans 15:4.)

The Story Of Creation Is Still True!

Even Christ could not have abolished the facts of the creation of all things as recorded in the book of beginnings called Genesis in the Old Testament, and well summarized by Moses in the Old Testament book called Exodus, which means "the road out," when he wrote, "For in six days the Lord made the heavens and the earth, the sea, and all that is in them, and rested the seventh day. Therefore the Lord blessed the Sabbath Day and hallowed it." (Exodus 20:11.)

Even though multitudes deny the sacred record of the creation of all things in the Old Testament as well as in the New Testament, because of their obsession with the evolutionary hypothesis, not anyone has proven that what the Bible says about the origin of all things is not so!

One of the leading advocates of the evolutionary doctrine is Dr. Robert Jastrow. He is also one of the most widely recognized scientists in the world. One of his books is entitled *"Until The Sun Dies."* In it he gives many details of how he thinks evolution occurred. Then he asked what concrete evidence is there that what he said is true. He answered his own question in the next sentence by saying, "There is none." (Page 72.) Dr. Jastrow goes on to say evolution instead of being science is a faith.

Scientists who reject what the Bible says about the origin of all things cannot tell us how things came to be except by expressing opinions or telling myths and legends about origins. The origin of things is not in the realm of natural science, but in the realm of faith, just as Dr. Jastrow said. If one does not <u>believe</u> what the Bible says about origins, he may <u>believe</u> the speculations on that subject that men have made. In either case it is faith. Faith in what the Bible says is well grounded. Faith in evolution rests in myths and wishful thinking!

If the Bible is the word of God; if it was written by men who were guided by Almighty God to write what they wrote in the Bible, then whatever the Bible says is so! It is much easier to believe what the Bible says about origins than it is to believe the myths and assumptions of men about how everything got started.

For more information on this important subject and many good reliable and sensible reasons for believing what the Bible teaches about the origin of all things, read my book entitled: *Evolution In The Light Of Scripture, Science And Sense.* There are many other books on this matter that are available.

Even though it is said in the Old Testament, it is just as true as ever that a universal flood came upon the earth when Noah and his family lived. It is just as true as ever that, by God's help, Moses led the children of Israel across the dry ground through the Red Sea.

The story of Jonah being swallowed by a great fish that God prepared, is still true even though it is in the Old Testament. If you have questions of doubt about this amazing "great fish" story, I highly recommend that you read a classic book written by the distinguished Christian scholar, J.W. McGarvey, entitled: *Jesus and Jonah.* It has been reported that after brother McGarvey died in 1911, *The London Times* newspaper in London, England, published a front-page article which said that J. W. McGarvey, the greatest Bible scholar in the English speaking world had died in Lexington, Kentucky.

Many Great And Eternal Principles

There is a multitude of eternal and unchanging principles taught in the Old Testament. It is still true that the man is blessed who does not walk in the counsel of the ungodly, and does not stand in the path of sinners, and does not sit in the seat of the scornful. (Psalm 1:1.)

It is still true that the way of transgressors is hard, even though that is stated in the Old Testament. (Proverbs 13:15.)

"The fear of the Lord is the beginning of knowledge, but fools despise wisdom and instruction." (Proverbs 1:7.) "The fear of the Lord is the beginning of wisdom, and the knowledge of the Holy One is understanding." (Proverbs 9:10.) "A good name is to be chosen rather than great riches, loving favor rather than silver and gold." (Proverbs 22:1.)

Another gem for good living is, "Hear my son and be wise; and guide your heart in the way. Do not mix with winebibbers, or with gluttonous eaters of meat; for the drunkard and the glutton will come to poverty, and drowsiness will clothe a man with rags." (Proverbs 23:19-21.)

"Do not boast about tomorrow, for you do not know what a day may bring forth. Let another praise you, and not your own mouth; a stranger and not your own lips." (Proverbs 27:1,2.)

"One who turns away his ear from hearing the law, even his prayer shall be an abomination." (Proverbs 28:9.)

"A man's pride will bring him low, but the humble in spirit will retain honor." (Proverbs 29:23.)

"Every word of God is pure; He is a shield to them who put their trust in him. Do not add to His words, lest He reprove you, and you be found a liar." (Proverbs 30:5,6.)

The foregoing gems of life and treasures of living are only a few of such in the book of Proverbs. Even though they are in the Old Testament, the Lord did not abolish them when He died on Calvary!

"I will praise You, for I am fearfully and wonderfully made: marvelous are your works, and that my soul knows very well." (Psalm 139:14.) We are indeed still fearfully and wonderfully made, and we should praise our God who made us!

There are many great principles about life, how not to live, and how to live, that are taught in the Old Testament book of Ecclesiastes which certainly were not abolished when Christ died on Calvary. In this part of the Old Testament, the wise man Solomon emphasized that riches, power, pleasure, and knowledge are vanity and vexation of spirit, without God. He even said childhood and youth are vanity if young people think that life is just doing what they please, and always having their way.

The wise man closed the book by writing, "Let us hear the conclusion of the whole matter: fear God and keep His commandments, for this is the whole duty of man. For God will bring every work into judgment, including every secret thing, whether it is good or whether it is evil." (Ecclesiastes 12:13,14.)

This solemn, searching, serious conclusion summarizes what life is really all about, and that is, live all the time with a clear sense and awareness of God and His awesomeness, and listen to Him in His word, and do what He says! This keeps life from being vanity and vexation of spirit. Jesus did not abolish this great unchanging principle of life and living when He died on Calvary!

Old Testament Messianic Prophecies

It is not within the purpose of this book to present an exhaustive treatment of the prophecies of Christ in the Old Testament. Many good books have been written on that subject.

One of those books was written by Homer Hailey, entitled, *The Messiah of Prophecy*, which contains 283 pages and was published in 1995 by Religious Supply, Inc. in Louisville, KY.

I was a student in some of brother Hailey's classes at Abilene Christian College in 1949-50. He was one of the best teachers I ever had. He resided with me and my family while he preached in a series of gospel meetings in 1955 at Murrell Boulevard Church of Christ in Paducah, KY where I was the regular preacher. Homer had been the preacher for the church in Honolulu. While he was with us the congregation there was needing a preacher. He tried to get me to go to that work, but I had already committed myself to do mission work in Richmond, KY where the church of Christ had eleven members, so we did not go to Honolulu. I had worshiped a number of times during my time in the U.S. Navy with the Honolulu church, and I think I would have enjoyed evangelizing there.

I wrote Homer a letter in the year 2000. He soon replied with a nice letter in which he said he was 97. He died soon thereafter. I did not always agree with him. I well recall his saying in class, with a humorous tone, "Overton was born disputing!" I loved Homer Hailey and admired him for his sincerity and scholarship.

Brother Hailey wrote many books. His book on *The Messiah of Prophecy* has three main parts. Part One contains 13 chapters which are titled: (1) The Seed Of The Woman; (2) The Seed Of Abraham, Isaac, and Jacob; (3) Judah The Tribe Selected; (4) The Seed – A Prophet; (5) The House Of David; (6) David's Messianic Psalms; (7) The Non-writing Prophets – The Divided Kingdom, 930-722 B.C.; (8) Ninth Century Prophets – Obadiah and Joel; (9) Eighth Century Prophets- Israel; (10) Eighth Century Prophets – Judah; (11) Seventh Century Prophets; (12) Sixth Century Prophets; and (13) Late Sixth and Fifth Century Prophets.

Part Two – The Messiah In The Flesh, consists of one chapter: "Lo, I Am Come."

Part Three – The Messiah On His throne consists of one chapter: Messianic Rule.

Another book on prophecies concerning Christ in the Old Testament is entitled *Messianic Prophecy* by Charles A. Briggs, D.D. and contains 519 pages. It was published in 1988 by Hendrickson Publishers in Peabody, MA.

All The Messianic Prophecies Of The Bible, by Herbert Lockyer with 528 pages was published by Zondervan Publishing Company in Grand Rapids, MI, in 1973. Lockyer's book contains 18 chapters. Seven of them deal with Old Testament prophecies of Christ as follows: (1) His Birth; (2) His Character; (3) His Ministry; (4) His Dual Nature; (5) His Death; (6) His Resurrection; and (7) His Ascension.

There being so many prophecies in the Old Testament about Christ, it is no wonder that the beloved physician, Luke wrote the following about the work of Paul and Silas!

"Now when they had passed through Amphipolis and Appolonia, they came to Thessalonica, where there was a synagogue of the Jews. Then Paul, as his custom was, went in to them, and for three Sabbaths reasoned with them from the Scriptures, explaining and demonstrating that the Christ had to suffer and rise again from the dead, and saying, 'This Jesus whom I preach to you is the Christ.' And some of them were persuaded; and a great multitude of the devout Greeks, and not a few of the leading women, joined Paul and Silas." (Acts 17:1-4.)

"The Scriptures" from which Paul "reasoned with them" were Old Testament Scriptures, and Paul used Messianic prophecies in those Scriptures in his "explaining and demonstrating that the Christ had to suffer and rise again from the dead" and that "This Jesus whom I preach to you is the Christ" or the Messiah!

I would very much like for our Jewish friends who do not believe Jesus is the Messiah, to tell us of whom Isaiah prophesied in his proleptic prophesy in chapter 53 of his Old Testament book, if he did not refer to Jesus Christ! I do not believe they can explain to whom Isaiah referred if he did not refer to Jesus Christ!

I first heard Hugo McCord preach about 65 years ago. He has a Ph.D. degree and is a Bible scholar. He is retired from preaching and is 91 years of age. He still writes a lot. I have published many of his articles in *The World Evangelist*. He sends me articles about every week. The following portion of one of his recent articles is indeed a fitting climax to the foregoing on the Old Testament prophesies concerning Jesus our Lord.

"In the Old Testament three hundred and thirty two predictions of the coming of Jesus have been counted (Floyd E. Hamilton, *The Basis Of The Christian Faith*, p. 157). Three hundred and thirty two pieces of marble, assembled by many different sculptors over some 1500 years, most of whom never saw one another, could not produce a beautiful statue, but only something ugly, fantastic, and grotesque.

"However, if a super-overseer sent out a plan for the three hundred and thirty two pieces of marble to local sculptors, the result would be a beautiful statue. So, God, as a super-overseer, sent out 'pure words, as silver tried in a furnace on the earth, purified seven times'" (Psalm 12:6), words describing the most beautiful life ever in human flesh in 332 ways hundreds of years before he was born.

"Of the 332 Old Testament predictions about the coming of Christ, *Jesus' Biography In The Psalms* is restricted to the 21 passages in the book of Psalms certified in the New Testaments predictions, and to three others (Psalm 22:1; 24:7-10; 31:5) that are believed to be predictions."

Some Other Old Testament Prophecies

There are scores of prophecies in the Old Testament about nations, and the Messiah and His kingdom or church. These are not part of the Law of Moses in the technical sense and could not be said to be part of what was abolished when Jesus died on Calvary. The following are some of these prophecies.

"And Babylon, the glory of kingdoms, the beauty of the Chaldees excellency, shall be as when God overthrew Sodom and Gomorrah. It shall never be inhabited, neither shall it be dwelt in from generation to generation: neither shall the Arabian pitch tent there; neither shall the shepherds make their fold there. But wild beasts of the desert shall lie there; and their houses shall be full of doleful creatures; and owls shall dwell there, and satyrs shall dance there. And the wild beasts of the islands shall cry in their desolate houses, and dragons in their pleasant palaces; and her time is near to come, and her days shall not be prolonged." (Isaiah 13:19-22.)

According to scholars, this prophecy began to be fulfilled when Babylon, despite its being "the beauty of the Chaldees excellency," fell about 180 years after God directed Isaiah to announce its doom. The many details of what Isaiah said would happen to this magnanimous and magnificent city were fulfilled gradually through many centuries, so that *Nelson's New Illustrated Bible Dictionary* says "Today, the ruins of this city stand as an eloquent testimony to the passing of proud empires and the providential hand of God." (page 149.)

God also directed Isaiah to prophesy the doom of Damascus with equal precision. (Chapter 17.) He also foretold the fall of Ethiopia (Chapter 18); Arabia (Chapter 21): Jerusalem (Chapter 22); Tyre (Chapter 23); and other places.

Isaiah also foretold the coming of the gospel, the establishment of His house or church in Jerusalem. (Chapter 2.) He prophesied the virgin birth of Christ (7:14) and the coming of that Messiah and His church or kingdom and its government, and His suffering and death for us. (9:6,7; 53.)

What Jesus Did Abolish

When Jesus died on the cross He abolished the Law of Moses, which means the law that instructed His children who lived under it on how they were children of God, and how they were to worship Him. That law included the ten commandments God gave to Moses on Mount Sinai. In Chapter Nine I presented some of the abundance of biblical evidence that the ten commandment law was abolished, and that nine of them are in the New Covenant or the gospel, along with many laws that were not in the ten commandments. The moral code in the gospel exceeds the moral code in the ten commandments of the Law of Moses.

Questions And Discussion Points

What does the chapter say about Dr. Robert Jastrow? Discuss.

What is said in the chapter about J. W. McGarvey?

Discuss some of the eternal principles in the Old Testament.

Discuss Ecclesiastes 12:13,14.

How can we make life not be vanity and vexation of Spirit?

Discuss Homer Hailey's book on *The Messiah of Prophesy*.

What are the titles of seven of the chapters in Herbert Lockyer's book?

Discuss the quotation from Hugo McCord.

Chapter Ten

WERE THERE TWO LAWS?

Seventh Day Adventists say that we are supposed to keep the seventh day Sabbath because one of the ten commandments tells us to. They say the ten commandments are the law of the Lord, or the law of God, and that it has not been abolished. They say there was another law called the law of Moses, the ceremonial law, that was abolished when Jesus died.

Seventh Day Adventists have many good teachings, but they are wrong when they say the Law of God and the Law of Moses were two different laws. Their attempts to prove this are vain. One reason for my saying this is that Chapters 8 and 9 of the Old Testament book called Nehemiah clearly teach that the Law of God and the Law of Moses were the same!

"Now all the people gathered together as one man in the open square that was in front of the Water Gate; and they told Ezra the scribe to bring the <u>Book of the Law of Moses</u>, which the Lord had commanded Israel. So Ezra the priest brought <u>the Law</u> before the congregation, of men and women and all who could hear with understanding, on the first day of the seventh month." (Nehemiah 8:1.)

What is called "<u>the Book of the Law of Moses</u>," and "<u>the Law</u>" in these verses, is called "<u>the Book of the Law</u>" in verse 3. The same Law is called "the book" in verse 5. Thirteen men are named in verse 8, and verse 9 says they and the Levites "read distinctly from the book in <u>the Law of God</u>, and they gave the sense, and helped them to understand the reading."

In these verses we easily learn that "<u>the Book of the Law of Moses</u>," and "<u>the Law of God</u>" are the same law. In verses 9, 13, and 14, "<u>the words of the Law</u>," and "<u>the Law, which the Lord had commanded by Moses</u>," refer to the same law. That same law is called "<u>the Book of the Law of God</u>, in verse 18, and in the next chapter in verse 3, it is called "<u>the Book of the Law of the Lord their God</u>."

More evidence that our Adventist friends are wrong in their vain efforts to make a distinction in "the law of the Lord" and "the law of Moses" is seen in 1 Chronicles 16:40 which tells us that burnt offerings were made "regularly morning and evening, and to do all that is written in the law of the Lord which he commanded Israel." This passage and its context prove that offering burnt offerings which was ceremonial was done according to "the law of the Lord" which Adventists say was done, not according to "the law of the Lord," but by "the law of Moses" which was the ceremonial law.

"And when eight days were completed for the circumcision of the Child, His name was called Jesus, the name given by the angel before He was conceived in the womb. Now when the days of her purification according to the law of Moses were completed, they brought Him to Jerusalem to present Him to the Lord (as it is written in the law of the Lord, 'Every male who opens the womb shall be called holy to the Lord'), and to offer a sacrifice according to what is said in the law of the Lord, 'A pair of turtledoves or two young pigeons.'" (Luke 2:21-24.)

Please observe that in the foregoing, the inspired writer, Luke, did not explain that "the Law of Moses" and "the law of the Lord" are two different laws. He used the two terms interchangeably which means they refer to the same law.

The apostle Paul very plainly taught in Romans 7:4-7 that the ten commandment law was abolished, and that those who had been under it were dead to it and delivered from it! We know he meant the ten commandment law because he quoted the tenth of the ten commandments which says, "Thou shalt not covet" to prove he meant the ten commandment law!

Of course this does not mean we are allowed under the new covenant to covet, because we are taught in the New Testament not to covet!

"And God blessed the seventh day and sanctified it: because that in it he had rested from all his work which God created and made." (Genesis 2:3.) Seventh Day Adventists use this scripture to try to prove that God's people observed the seventh day sabbath from the time of the creation. But this text does not teach this. When Moses wrote this about 1400 B.C. he did not say when God sanctified the seventh day, but he told why he did, and that was because "in it he had rested." Sometime after God had rested he sanctified the seventh day, but he told why he did, and that was because "in it he had rested." Sometime after God had rested he sanctified the seventh day. He did it when he gave the law of Moses. Nehemiah 9:13,14 says that on Mount Sinai God made known the sabbath day to his people!

Just prior to the formal making known of the Sabbath day in the ten commandments law, according to Exodus chapter 16, the Lord through Moses gave detailed instructions to the people on how to observe the seventh day Sabbath because it was something completely new to them. Look again at Exodus 20:8-11 where the command to keep the seventh day Sabbath was given as the fourth of the ten commandments and you will see the details God gave on how to keep that sabbath. He did this because it was something new to the people!

There is no record in the Bible that anyone kept the seventh day sabbath, or even knew about it before Moses led the Israelites out of Egypt!

Seventh Day Adventists also teach that in the fourth century A.D., the Roman Emperor Constantine changed the day of worship from the seventh day to the first day of the week. This is not true. Constantine merely gave official state recognition to the day on which the Christians were already worshiping which was Sunday or the first day of the week. History shows they had been worshiping on the first day of the week since the days of the writers of the New Testament!

"Therefore the children of Israel shall keep the Sabbath, to observe the Sabbath throughout their generations as a perpetual covenant." (Exodus 31:16.) Sabbatarians misuse this scripture to try to prove the law regarding the keeping of the Sabbath was never to cease, because it was perpetual. The next verse says God said the Sabbath "...is a sign between Me and the children of Israel forever...." "Forever" obviously is the same as "throughout their generations," and it did not involve our Seventh Day Adventist neighbors because it was to be done because God says it was a sign between Him and the children of Israel. "Their generations" or the Jewish Age closed at the crucifixion of Jesus. Furthermore, our Sabbatarian friends are inconsistent because in Exodus 30:8, the Bible says, "And when Aaron lights the lamps at twilight, he shall burn incense on it, a perpetual incense before the Lord throughout your generations."

The Sabbatarians say the burning of incense was part of the ceremonial law (the Law of Moses) which was done away when Jesus died. This means they do not think "perpetual" means that it would never cease!

Sabbath For The Israelites Only

The law to keep the seventh day Sabbath was never given to any except the Israelites. The Lord said so!

"Therefore I made them go out of the land of Egypt and brought them into the wilderness. And I gave them My statutes and showed them My judgments, 'which, if a man does, he shall live by them.' Moreover I also gave them My Sabbaths, to be a sign between them and Me, that they might know that I am the Lord who sanctifies them. But I said to their children in the wilderness, 'Do not walk in the statutes of your fathers, nor observe their judgments, nor defile yourselves with their idols. I am the Lord your God: walk in My statutes, keep My judgments, and do them; hallow My Sabbaths, and they will be a sign between Me and you, that you may know that I am the Lord your God.' Notwithstanding, the children rebelled against Me; they did not walk in My statutes, and were not careful to observe My judgments, which, if a man does, he shall live by them; but they profaned My Sabbaths. Then I said I would pour out My fury on them and fulfill My anger against them in the wilderness." (Ezekiel 20:10-12; 18:21.)

The seventh day Sabbath was not the only Sabbath God ordered in the Law of Moses. There were other Sabbaths including Sabbath years. Exodus 23 and Leviticus 23, 26, and 2 Chronicles 36 are some of the chapters which tell about these.

"Sabbath" does not mean "seventh," but is from Hebrew "shabbath" that means a rest. The Greek word "sabbtismos" in Hebrews 4:9 is translated "a rest," and there refers to the Sabbath of Christians which is Heaven. Under the New Covenant Christians worship on the first day of the week, the Lord's Day, which does not compare to the seventh day Sabbath of the Law of Moses.

The New Testament tells about Paul and others going in Jewish synagogues on the Jewish Sabbath day to teach the people who did not know that the Law of Moses had been abolished. After Paul did this in Corinth, Greece, the enraged Jews brought him before Gallio, the deputy of Achaia (Greece) and told him that Paul "persuadeth men to worship God contrary to the law." (Acts 18:13.) The context makes it clear they meant the Law of Moses! The apostle

Paul did not go into the synagogue in Corinth or any other place to observe the Jewish Sabbath.

In the thirteen or fourteen Epistles in the New Testament which the apostle Paul wrote, he mentioned the Jewish Sabbaths of the Law of Moses only one time and that is when he told Christians not to let anyone bind on them the keeping of them.

Are We Under Any Kind Of Law?

Some argue that since we are under grace in the reign of Christ, or in the gospel dispensation, therefore we are not under the law. However, Paul wrote, "For the grace of God that bringeth salvation hath appeared to all men, teaching us that, denying ungodliness and worldly lusts, we should live soberly, righteously, and godly, in this present world." (Titus 2:11,12.) This shows that being under grace that saves means we have restraints regarding bad conduct, and teaching regarding what we must do in order to live right. The grace of God that saves teaches us what not to do and what to do! Where does the grace of God teach these? The obvious answer to this question is, in the gospel, or in the new covenant or new testament which we have under Christ. This system of teaching is called "the law and the word of the Lord" in Isaiah 2:3 in the prophecy of the establishing of the house of God, or the church, and the giving of the new law or covenant on the first Pentecost following the resurrection of Christ.

In the prophecy concerning the new law in Jeremiah 31:31-34 God said, "I will put my law in their inward parts, and write it in their hearts...." This prophecy is interpreted by another inspired man in Hebrews chapters 8 and 10 as referring to the gospel of Christ. So, even in prophecy the gospel of grace is called God's law!

The New Testament teaches that the gospel or the new covenant contains a code of moral conduct. When Paul wrote in 1 Timothy 1:8 "the law is good if a man use it lawfully" he referred to the law of morality which is in the gospel, for he continued with the following. "Knowing this, that the law is not made for a righteous man, but for the lawless and disobedient, for the ungodly and for sinners, for unholy and profane, for murderers of fathers and murderers of mothers, for manslayers, for whoremongers, for them that defile themselves with mankind, for menstealers, for liars, for perjured persons, and if there be any other thing that is contrary to sound doctrine; according to the glorious gospel of the blessed God which is committed to my trust." (1 Timothy 1:9-11.)

This proves that all such immoral and criminal conduct is contrary to the gospel! This means the gospel contains God's law regarding moral conduct! It also shows how important it is to teach the sound or healthy doctrine concerning proper conduct which is in the gospel.

Doctrine means teaching. For crime to be stopped, the sound doctrine concerning proper conduct which is in the gospel must be taught and practiced.

Paul wrote of Christ's law of conduct when he wrote, "Bear ye one another's burdens, and so fulfill the law of Christ." (Galatians 6:2.)

James wrote of the engrafted word which is able to save our souls which is the gospel, and he said being a doer of that word and not just a hearer was continuing in "the perfect law of liberty." (James 1:21-25.)

Questions And Discussion Points

Discuss Nehemiah chapter eight.

Discuss 1 Chronicles 16:40.

Discuss Luke 2:21-24.

Discuss Romans 7:1-4.

When did God sanctify the seventh day according to Nehemiah 9:13,14?

How does Exodus chapter 16 prove Sabbath keeping new to the children of Israel?

Does the Bible say anyone knew about the seventh day Sabbath before Moses led the Israelites out of Egypt?

Did the Roman Emperor Constantine change the day of worship from the seventh day (sabbath) to the first day of the week (Sunday)?

Chapter Eleven

OLD COVENANT WORSHIP INCLUDED SINGING, INSTRUMENTAL MUSIC, ANIMAL SACRIFICES, AND BURNT OFFERINGS

The worship practices of those under the Old Covenant were not limited to just what God ordained through Moses, but also included things said by other prophets of God. Sometimes the Old Covenant is referred to in a general way as "the law of Moses," and sometimes as "the law and the prophets" as in Luke 16:1; Acts 13:15; 24:14; and Romans 3:21. Sometimes the "old covenant" is called "the first covenant" in contrast with "the new covenant" as in Hebrews 9:15.

The ten commandments were only a part of the law God gave through Moses and the prophets. That law also contained laws about the offering of sacrifices and many other matters pertaining to the worship God's people rendered to Him under that law. The following portion of the Old Testament is an example of how elaborate, complex, costly, and arduous the worship was, which the Almighty authorized under the old covenant.

"Then King Hezekiah rose early, gathered the rulers of the city, and went up to the house of the Lord. And they brought seven bulls, seven rams, seven lambs, and seven male goats for a sin offering for the kingdom, for the sanctuary, and for Judah. Then he commanded the priests, the sons of Aaron, to offer them on the altar of the Lord. So they killed the bulls, and the priests received the blood and sprinkled it on the altar. Likewise they killed the rams and sprinkled the blood on the altar. Then they brought out the male goats for the sin offering before the king and the congregation, and they laid their hands on them. And the priests killed them; and they presented their blood on the altar as a sin offering to make an atonement for all Israel, for the king commanded that the burnt

offering and the sin offering be made for all Israel. Then he stationed the Levites in the house of the Lord with cymbals, with stringed instruments, and with harps, according to the commandment of David, of Gad the king's seer, and of Nathan the prophet; <u>for thus was the commandment of the Lord by his prophets</u>.

"The Levites stood with the instruments of David, and the priests with the trumpets. Then Hezekiah commanded them to offer the burnt offering on the altar. And when the burnt offering began, the song of the Lord also began, with the trumpets and with the instruments of David king of Israel. So all the congregation worshiped, the singers sang, and the trumpeters sounded; all this continued until the burnt offering was finished. And when they had finished offering, the king and all who were present with him bowed and worshiped. Moreover King Hezekiah and the leaders commanded the Levites to sing praise to the Lord with the words of David and of Asaph the seer. So they sang praises with gladness, and they bowed their heads and worshiped.

"Then Hezekiah answered and said, 'Now that you have consecrated yourselves to the Lord, come near, and bring sacrifices and thank offerings into the house of the Lord.' So the congregation brought in sacrifices and thank offerings, and as many as were of a willing heart brought burnt offerings. And the number of the burnt offerings which the congregation brought was seventy bulls, one hundred rams, and two hundred lambs; all these were for a burnt offering to the Lord. The consecrated things were six hundred bulls and three thousand sheep. But the priests were too few, so that they could not skin all the burnt offerings; therefore their brethren the Levites helped them until the work was ended and until the other priests had sanctified themselves, for the Levites were more diligent in sanctifying themselves than the priests. Also the burnt offerings were in abundance, with the fat of the peace offerings and with the drink offerings for every burnt offering. So the service of the house of the Lord was set in order. Then Hezekiah and all the people rejoiced that God had prepared the people, since the events took place so suddenly." (2 Chronicles 29:20:36.)

More about worship under the Law of Moses is in the next chapter of 2 Chronicles in verses 21 and 22 which say, "So the children of Israel who were present in Jerusalem kept the Feast of Unleavened Bread seven days with great gladness; and the Levites and the priests praised the Lord day by day, singing to the Lord, accompanied by loud instruments. And Hezekiah gave encouragement to all the Levites who taught the good knowledge for the Lord; and they ate throughout the feast seven days, offering peace offerings and making confession to the Lord God of their fathers."

"According To The Commandment Of The Lord"

Please observe that the worship of those people under the Law of Moses was according to "the commandment of the Lord by his prophets," and it included the use of instruments of music! (29:25-28.) Some try to justify the use of instruments in worship in the gospel age, or under the new covenant by citing the foregoing scriptures, and other Old Testament Scriptures that say mechanical instruments of music were used in worship under the law of Moses. This is a misuse of Holy Scripture because that law was abolished in the death of Christ!

Primary Purpose Of Hebrews

The New Testament Book of Hebrews was written primarily to show the difference in the Law of Moses and the New Covenant which is the gospel of our Lord Jesus. The following is a sample of the many things it says about this distinction.

"For when Moses had spoken every precept to all the people according to the law, he took the blood of calves and goats, with water, scarlet wool, and hyssop, and sprinkled both the book itself and all the people, saying, 'This is the blood of the covenant, which God has commanded you.' Then likewise he sprinkled with blood both the tabernacle and all the vessels of the ministry. And according to the law almost all things are purged with blood, and without shedding of blood there is no remission. Therefore it was necessary that the copies of the things in the heavens should be purified with these, but the heavenly things themselves with better sacrifices than these. For Christ has not entered the holy places made with hands, which are copies of the true, but into heaven itself, now to appear in the presence of God for us; not that He should offer Himself often, as the high priest enters the Most Holy Place every year with blood of another – He then would have had to suffer often since the foundation of the world; but now, once at the end of the ages, He has appeared to put away sin by the sacrifice of Himself. And as it is appointed for men to die once, but after this the judgment, so Christ was offered once to bear the sins of many. To those who eagerly wait for Him He will appear a second time, apart from sin, for salvation." (Hebrews 9:19-28.)

"For the law, having a shadow of the good things to come, and not the very image of the things, can never with these same sacrifices, which they offer continually year by year, make those who approach perfect. For then would they not have ceased to be offered? For worshipers, once purged, would have had no more consciousness of sins.

But in those sacrifices there is a reminder of sins every year. For it is not possible that the blood of bulls and goats could take away sins. Therefore, when He came into the world, He said: Sacrifice and offering You did not desire, But a body You have prepared for Me. In burnt offerings and sacrifices for sin You had no pleasure. Then I said, 'Behold, I have come – In the volume of the book it is written of Me – To do Your will, O God.'" (Hebrews 10:1-7.)

The practices enumerated in the foregoing Scriptures from 2 Chronicles and Hebrews that were involved in worship under the old covenant were abolished when Jesus abolished that covenant when he died on Calvary. (Ephesians 2:11-16; Colossians 2:13,14.) Worship enjoined by the good Lord in His new covenant recorded in the New Testament must be "in spirit and in truth." (John 4:24.)

Someone might say, "There was singing in the old covenant worship, are we to conclude that singing in worship was done away?" The answer is, singing with instrumental music and burnt offerings was done away when the old covenant was abolished. The new covenant authorizes singing, but not with burnt offerings and instrumental music!

Instrumental music in Christian worship is no more scriptural than burnt offerings in Christian worship! Neither is authorized in the New Testament!

The New Testament commands Christians to sing, not with burnt offerings and/or instrumental music, but by "making melody in your heart to the Lord" (Ephesians 5:19); and "with grace in your heart to the Lord." (Colossians 3:16.)

Some try to justify the use of instrumental music in worship under the new covenant even though they know such is not authorized in the New Testament. They say playing of instruments in worship is just an aid to worship by singing. Then they use what is said in the Old Testament about the use of instrumental music in worship to try to support their position. Please notice above in 2 Chronicles 29 that "all the congregation worshiped, the singers sang, and the trumpeters sounded; all this continued until the burnt offering was finished." The ones who played the musical instruments worshiped! What they did was not an aid to worship, it was worship!

The worship practices commanded in the old covenant were abolished when Jesus abolished that law of which they were a part, when he died on Calvary. (Ephesians 2:11-16; Colossians 2:13,14.) These practices in worship are not enjoined upon God's people in Christian worship which is the worship that is sealed by the blood of Christ, and must be "in spirit and in truth," according to Him. (John 4:23-25.)

Questions And Discussion Points

Discuss some laws of the Law of Moses which were not in the ten commandments.

Discuss what the chapter says about what King Hezekiah did.

What is in 2 Chronicles 29:25-28?

What is the primary purpose of the Book of Hebrews?

What kinds of blood did Moses sprinkle on the book of the law and all the people?

Discuss other matters in Hebrews 9:19-28.

Discuss Hebrews 10:1-7.

Discuss burnt offerings and instrumental music in Old Testament worship.

Chapter Twelve

WHO INVENTED FOR THEMSELVES
MUSICAL INSTRUMENTS LIKE DAVID?

"Woe to you who are at ease in Zion, and trust in Mount Samaria, notable persons in the chief nation, to whom the house of Israel comes! Go over to Calneh and see; and from there go to Hamath the great; then go down to Gath of the Philistines. Are you better than these kingdoms? Or is their territory greater than your territory? Woe to you who put far off the day of doom, who cause the seat of violence to come near; who lie on beds of ivory, stretch out on your couches, eat lambs from the flock and calves from the midst of the stall; who chant to the sound of stringed instruments, and invent for yourselves musical instruments like David; who drink wine from bowls, and anoint yourselves with the best ointments, but are not grieved for the affliction of Joseph.

Therefore they shall now go captive as the first of the captives, and those who recline at banquets shall be removed. The Lord God has sworn by Himself, the Lord God of hosts says: I abhor the pride of Jacob, and hate his palaces; therefore I will deliver up the city and all that is in it." (Amos 6:1-8.)

Some cite a portion of the foregoing to try to prove David sinned by authorizing the use of instruments of music in the worship of people who were under the Law of Moses. However, all need to understand that David did this because it was "the commandment of the Lord by his prophets." (2 Chronicles 29:25.) A prophet was one who was inspired and spoke for God. David was a prophet, but he was not the only prophet who authorized the use of instruments of music in Old Testament worship, because 2 Chronicles 29:25 says the Lord's prophets (plural) commanded its use.

Some say God did not authorize instrumental music in old covenant worship because 2 Chronicles 29:25,26 refers to their use as "according to the commandment of David," and as "the instruments of David." However, the text makes it clear that David commanded their use because it "was the commandment of the Lord." Surely no one thinks that "the law of Moses" means that law was not God's law! "Law of Moses" does not mean that law originated with Moses neither does "commandment of David" mean that commandment originated with David.

We accept as authoritative what inspired men wrote and commanded in the New Testament, because we believe they wrote and commanded what the Lord commanded.

When the context of Amos 6 is carefully considered we can easily see that it is a misuse of the passage to say it means that David did wrong because he authorized instruments of music in worship. Under the old covenant he used them in worship because the Lord commanded their use in praising God as in Psalm 150.

Amos wrote his Old Testament book about 300 years after David lived. Amos pronounced woe upon some in Israel because of their sacrilegious and luxurious practices which included licentious laziness and lethargy. They used musical instruments in their entertaining and revellous practices as David and others had used them in worshiping and praising God, as God had commanded!

The picture in Amos 6 is a portrayal of wantonness, and conduct that encouraged people to sin. It is a picture of indolence that encouraged laziness. It is a scene of lolling in luxury. They lay "upon beds of ivory." The following comments on Amos 6 from *Pulpit Commentary*, Volume 14, page 113 is very appropriate here.

"As David devised stringed instruments and modes of singing to do honour to God and for the service of his sanctuary (see 1 Chronicles 15:16, etc.; 23:5; 2 Chronicles 29:26,27; and the supernumerary psalm at the end of the Psalter in the Septuagint), so these debauchees invented new singing and playing to grace their luxurious feasts."

The following is also very fitting here.

"Luxury is a direct result of indolence. Having nothing else to occupy their attention, men concentrate it on themselves. They make it the business of their life to coddle themselves, with the inevitable result of becoming harder to please. As the appetite is pampered it becomes more dainty, and must be tempted with luxury after luxury, if any measure of relish would be retained.... The tendency of luxury is to unman. On the discontinuance of manly exercises follows closely the loss of manly qualities. Pampering the body weakens body and mind both, and prepares the way for occupations that will be in character. Effeminacy grows fastest when nursed in the lap of luxury. The Israel that was too fastidious to lie on anything but an ivory couch, or too dainty to touch coarser fare than the fatted calf, was too enervated in a little while for any manlier pastime than trilling to a harp." (*Pulpit Commentary*, Volume 14, page 116.)

The following comments by Matthew Henry on the people Amos 6:1-7 describes are very insightful. He said of them, "… they gave themselves up to their pleasures, spent their time in them, and threw away their thoughts, and cares, and estates, upon them; they were in these enjoyments as in their element; their hearts were upon them, they exceeded all bounds in them, and this at a time when God in his providence was calling them to weeping and mourning; (Isaiah 22:12,13) when they were under guilt and wrath, and the judgments of God were ready to break in upon them, they called for wine and strong drink, presuming that tomorrow shall be as this day, and much more abundant, (Isaiah 56:12) thus walking contrary to God, and setting his justice at defiance. (1) They were extravagant in their furniture; nothing would serve them but beds of ivory, to sleep upon, or to sit on at their meat, when sackcloth and ashes had better become them. (2) They were lazy, and humoured themselves in the love of ease; they did not only lie down, but stretched themselves upon their couches, when they should have stirred up themselves to their business; they were willingly slothful, and took a pride in doing nothing; they abounded in superfluities, (so the margin reads it,) when many of their poor brethren wanted necessaries. (3) They were nice and curious in their diet, must have every thing of the best, and abundance of it; they eat the lambs out of the flock, (lambs by wholesale), and the calves out of the midst of the stall, the fattest they could lay their hand on; and these perhaps not out of their own flock and their own stall, but taken by oppression from the poor. (4) They were merry and jovial, and diverted themselves at their feasts with music and singing; they chant to the sound of the viol, sing and play in concert, and they invent new-fashioned instruments of music, striving herein, more than in any thing else, to excel their ancestors; they set their wits on work to contrive how to please their fancy. Some men never show their ingenuity but in their luxury; on that they bestow all their faculty of invention and contrivance. They invent instruments of music, like David; entertain themselves with that which formerly used to be the entertainment of kings only. Or, it intimates their profaneness in their mirth; they mimicked the temple-music, and made a jest of that, because, it may be, it was old-fashioned, and they took a pride in bantering it, as the Babylonians did when they urged the captives to sing them the songs of Zion; such was Belshazzar's profaneness, when he drank wine in temple-bowls, and such theirs that sing vain and loose songs in psalm-tunes, on purpose to ridicule a divine institution. (5) They drink to excess, and never think they can pour down enough; they drink wine in bowls, not in glasses or cups; (as Jeremiah 35:5) they hate to be stinted, and must have large draughts, and therefore make use of vessels, that they can steal a draught out of. (6) They affect the strongest perfumes; they anoint themselves with the chief ointments, to please the smell, and to make them more in love with their own bodies, and to guard against those presages of putrefaction, which they carry about with them while they live. No ordinary ointments would serve their turn; they must have the chief, such as were far-fetched, and dear-bought, when cheaper would have served as well."

The foregoing is from Volume IV, pages 1372 and 1373 of *Matthew Henry's Commentary on the Bible*. He wrote six volumes containing 4,132 pages. The pages are 8 ? inches by 6 ? inches, and the print is relatively small. This was a monumental accomplishment, indeed. Mr. Henry was born in England October 18, 1662. They lose credibility who attempt to get around the fact that God through his prophets commanded the use of mechanical instruments of music in the worship under the Law of Moses. The fact that God commanded their use, and His people obeyed Him by using them in worship, strengthens the case for not using them in Christian worship, under the New Covenant of Christ. **Had God wanted Christians to use them in worship He would have commanded their use in the New Covenant under Christ just as He commanded their use in the worship under the Old Covenant, or Law of Moses!**

Insightful Information By Ayers

F. M. Green wrote a book entitled: *The Life And Times of John F. Rowe*, which was published in 1899. On pages 109-111, he recited as "unquestionably conclusive" an article by a Mr. Ayers on why Christian worship should not include the use of mechanical instruments of music. Be sure to read it all to sense how clearly devastating it is to the position that it is all right to use them in such worship. The article follows.

"1. Instrumental music was as common in the days of the Apostles as in the present day. It was used everywhere; in the temple, in the camp, on both festive and funeral occasions, and in the domestic circle, both among Jews and heathen; and, together with singing, was cultivated as an art by all nations and all people. It was ordained of God as a special part of the Temple worship at Jerusalem, and its cultivation and performance was especially assigned to the tribe of Levi and the sons of Aaron. (2 Samuel 5:5; 1 Chronicles 15, 25 and 27:11-13; 2 Chronicles 5:12-13; 29:25; Matthew 9:23); and for the domestic circle (Luke 5: 25); all this showing the vast number of musical instruments and the multitude of performers to play on them in Jerusalem and in all Judea.

"2. The Apostles in their writings alluded to this art as one of universal prevalence, not only among Jews, but also among the Gentiles; and to its practice and utility as a fact with which mankind were generally acquainted, insomuch as that, in illustrating certain points of church decorum and edification, they spoke of it thus: 'And even things without life giving sound, whether pipe or harp, except they give a distinction in the sounds, how shall we know what is piped or harped? For if the trumpet shall give an uncertain sound, who shall prepare himself to the battle? So likewise ye, except ye utter by the tongue words easy to be understood, how shall it be known what is spoken?'" (1 Corinthians 24:7-9).

"3. Not only some of the leading men of the church, eminent among the Apostles, had been connected with the musical instruments; but soon after Pentecost 'a great company of priests (sons of Aaron) became obedient to the faith,' who also were divinely appointed to blow on trumpets during the solemnities of the sacrifice. (Numbers 10:8,10; 2 Chronicles 5:12,13; Acts 4:36; 6:7.)

"4. It was furthermore, then, as now, that instrumental music was regarded universally as more agreeable and delightful than singing; and that at least singing, to have its best and most inspiring effect, must have its instrumental accompaniment. (1 Samuel 16:23; 1 Chronicles 15:16-28; 2 Chronicles 5:12,13.) All these being the verities of inspired history.

"**5. And yet that the Apostles, under all these circumstances, with all the allusions made to the universal practice of instru-**

mental music in their writings to the churches, and with all the above enumerated musical facilities at their command, should never in the whole sixty years of their labor and worship in the churches have played themselves, or had played by others on any instrument a single tune, either alone or as an accompaniment to Christian song; that they should also, by their several epistles in regard to the musical service of God, ignore the whole affair of instrumental music, pipe, trumpet, harp and organ, and specifically enjoin them to 'sing, making melody in their hearts to the Lord,' prescribing the simple, plain, unaffected congregational singing, 'grating and discordant' as it might be to the 'cultivated ear,' – that the Apostles should have thus acted is wholly irreconcilable with the idea that they ever intended instrumental music to be used in Christian worship.**

"These facts, then, fairly considered, bring us to these two conclusions, from which there is no escape:

"1. That, though we may think it 'very bad taste,' 'very old-fogyish,' and 'far behind the times,' and 'calculated to drive the young people away from the church,' and all that, yet that there was something about instrumental music which the Apostles regarded as improper, either in leading or accompanying Christian praise; and that their treatment of it thus (leaving 'parlor accomplishment' out of the view) amounts to nothing short of absolute prohibition so far as Christian praise is concerned – yesterday, to-day and forever!

"2. And that, in all questions of 'expediency' as to the lawful use of modern appliances to improve Christian singing, in the church or in the family, such as notebooks, tuning forks, troches, lozenges, etc., however these may be disposed of, the matter of instrumental music is wholly out of the question, since the art was everywhere present before the Apostles, and about them in Jerusalem, in all Judea and to the uttermost parts of the earth; and they calmly, quietly turned away from it, and persistently ignored it in all its forms and utilities…."

Questions And Discussion Points

Discuss how Amos 6:1-8 is misused by some.

Discuss the quotes in the chapter from *Pulpit Commentary*, and what Matthew Henry said.

How can one use the fact that God commanded the use of instruments in Old Testament worship, to prove God does not want them used in New Testament worship? Discuss.

What is the main thrust of what F. M. Green quoted from a Mr. Ayers?

Did Mr. Ayers say that in the days of Christ and his apostles instruments of music were not used anywhere? Discuss.

Are there references to musical instruments in the New Testament?

Did New Testament writers say musical instruments were used in church worship?

Discuss the last paragraph of what Mr. Ayers said.

Chapter Thirteen

WHY NOT WRITE A
BETTER BOOK?

Many years ago in Kentucky I had a friend who was a skeptic. He had a doctor's degree and taught in a great institution of higher learning. The last time I talked with him we discussed Christ and the Bible. He spoke against the Bible. I used on him something William Jennings Bryan used in talking with skeptics which was something like the following.

"The Bible was written by about 40 men over a period of more than 1500 years. You should find 39 other scholars like yourself, one from each of 39 colleges and universities. You 40 scholars should write a book, but not borrow anything from the Bible to go in it. You have spoken against the Bible, so do not write a book merely as good as the Bible for you have spoken against it. You need to write one better than the Bible."

After I had said that, my friend walked away with his face down and did not say anything. I never saw him again. He has long since met his Maker.

Who can write a book better than the Bible? No one! The Bible was written by men who were directed by their Maker.

Word Of God Or Word Of Men?

The distinguished scholar William Paley (1743-1805) was a superb defender of the Bible as the Word of God. He said, "Even so, to disbelieve the superhuman origin of the Bible, is to believe its human origin: and which belief demands the more easy faith, is the very point at issue." (William Paley, *A View Of The Evidences Of Christianity*, page 34. This book was republished in 1952 by my old friend George DeHoff.)

There are enormous and edifying implications in what Dr. Paley said. His statement motivated me many years ago to preach many times on "The Belief Of Unbelievers." I recommend that all preachers of the word do that.

If the Bible is not the Word of God it is the word of man. If it is the word of man, no one can rationally explain how uninspired men could have written such a book. If it was written by men whom God directed or inspired to write what they wrote, no other explaining is needed!

The following eloquent statements by Archibald Alexander should convince anyone why he should not expect a book better than the Bible to be written, and why it is easy to believe the Bible is not the word of men but the word of God!

"The question to be decided is, whether a book which is replete with such sublime and correct views of theology; which exhibits the true history and true character of man, without flattery, distortion, or exaggeration; which possesses such an astonishing power of penetrating the human heart and affecting the conscience; which gives us information on the very points with which it is more important we should be acquainted; which opens to us the future world, and shows us how we may attain its felicity and glory; which exhibits a perfect system of moral duty adapted to our nature and circumstances, and free from all the defects of other systems of morality; forbidding nothing which is innocent, and requiring nothing which is not reasonable and virtuous; which reduces all duty to a few general principles, and yet illustrates the application of these principles by a multitude of particular precepts, addressed to persons in every relation of life, and exemplifies them by setting before us the lives of holy men, who are portrayed according to truth with such imperfections as experience teaches us belong to the best men; which delineates the character of Jesus Christ, the founder of Christianity, with such a perfection of moral excellency, by simply relating his words, actions, and sufferings, that nothing can be taken from it, or added to it, without detracting from its worth; and finally, which contains the true sources of consolation for every species of human suffering, and comfort in death itself: whether such a book is the production of vile impostors, and those impostors uneducated fishermen. Would such men have fallen into no palpable blunders in theology or morality? Could they have preserved so beautiful a harmony and consistency between all the parts? Could they have exhibited such a character as that of Jesus Christ? And while they introduce him acting and speaking so often, and in circumstances so peculiar and difficult, never ascribe to him any error or weakness, in word or deed? Would impostors have denounced all manner of falsehood and deceit, as is done in the New Testament? Would they have insisted so much on holiness, even in the thoughts and purposes of the heart? Could they have so perfectly adapted their forgery to the constitution of the human mind and to the circumstances of men? Is it probable that they would have possessed the wisdom to avoid all the prejudices of their nation, and all connection with existing sects and civil institutions? And finally, could they have provided so effectually for the consolation of the afflicted? What man now upon earth could compose even the discourses, said by the evangelists to have been spoken by Jesus Christ?

"If any man can bring himself, after an impartial examination of the Scriptures, to believe that they were written by unprincipled impostors, then he may believe that an untutored savage might construct a ship of the line; that a child might have written the Iliad, or Paradise Lost; or even that the starry firmament was the work of mere creatures. No: it cannot be that this is a forgery. No man or set of men ever had sufficient talents and knowledge to forge such a book as the Bible. It evidently transcends all human effort. It has upon its face the impress of divinity. It shines with a light, which by its clearness and its splendour, shows itself to be celestial. It possesses the energy and penetrating influence which bespeak the omnipotence and omniscience of its author. It has the effect of enlightening, elevating, purifying, directing, and comforting all those who cordially receive it. Surely then it is the Word of God, and we hold it fast as the best blessing which God has vouchsafed to man.

"O precious gospel! Will any merciless hand endeavour to tear away from our hearts this best, this last, and sweetest consolation? Would you darken the only avenue through which one ray of hope can enter? Would you tear from the aged and infirm poor the only prop on which their souls can repose in peace? Would you deprive the dying of their only source of consolation? Would you rob the world of its richest treasure? Would you let loose the flood-gates of every vice, and bring back upon the earth the horrors of superstition or the atrocities of atheism? Then endeavour to subvert the gospel; throw around you the fire-bands of infidelity; laugh at religion, and make a mock of futurity; but be assured that for all these things God will bring you into judgment. But I will not believe that any who reflect on what has been said, in these pages, will ever cherish a thought so diabolical. I will persuade myself that a regard for the welfare of their country, if no higher motive, will induce them to respect the Christian religion. And every pious heart will say, rather let the light of the sun be extinguished than the precious light of the gospel." (*Alexander's Evidence of Christianity*, pages 219,220,221.)

Other Eloquent Testimony

Many years ago brother W. J. Russell magnified the Bible very eloquently in the following.

"The Bible is the ring that unites earth with heaven as the long, mild twilight like a silver clasp unites today with yesterday. And if you would destroy this grand old volume and its influence, you must destroy the largest and most valuable portion of the literature of the world. You must tear out the leaves that have any Bible in them from every book – everything that has been quoted, suggested, derived directly or indirectly from the Bible – every allusion to it in history; every metaphor drawn from it in poetry; every quotation and thought in romance, every idea incorporated in philosophy; every passage written to defend or illustrate it in science; every principle taken from it in law; every sentence that indicates any knowledge of the Bible must be cut out.

"The Bible is full of the choicest gems of thought, combining a variety and richness and rareness to be found in no other book. Would you have logic? Then turn to Paul's letter to the Ephesians or his discourse on Mars Hill, recorded in Acts of Apostles. Would you be moved by the sublime? Where shall we find it if not in Job, Isaiah, the Psalms and Revelation? Would you take time to meditate upon wise sayings or maxims? Where are these to be found, so full of pith and pungency, so terse, so sharp, so vigorous as in the Proverbs of Solomon? For a story of filial affection and devotion I refer you to the book of Ruth – that book which Voltaire said was beyond anything found in Homer or in any other classic writers." (W. J. Russell: *New Testament Christianity*, Vol., II, Edited by Z. T. Sweeney; pages 358, 359; 1926.)

The great Christian scholar, J. W. McGarvey was a very effective defender of the Bible as the Word of God. The following is a small sample of his monumental efforts.

"We invite attention next to the air of infallibility which the writers of both Testaments everywhere assume. Though they speak on some themes which have baffled the powers of all thinkers, such as the nature of God, his eternal purposes, his present will, angels, disembodied human spirits, the introduction of sin, the forgiveness and punishment of sin, the future of this earth, and the eternal destiny of us all; on all subjects and on all occasions they speak with a confidence which knows no hesitation, and which admits no possibility of a mistake.

"Was this the result of stupidity and of overweening self-consciousness? The fact that they are still the teachers of the world on these themes forbids the supposition. Was it the result of a profundity of learning never equaled, or of native powers of insight never approached by the genius of other men?

"Their positions in society and their want of favorable opportunities forbid this supposition, and our opponents themselves are quick to reject it. What then shall we claim as the cause of it? Grant their miraculous inspiration, and all is plain. There is no other rational hypothesis." (J. W. McGarvey, *Sermons Delivered In Louisville, Kentucky*, page 12; Christian Standard Publishing Co., 1894.)

It pleases me to include part of a sermon by N. B. Hardeman, at whose feet I sat three years at Freed-Hardeman College (now University) 1946-1949. He and I corresponded many years. I never wrote him a letter he did not answer. I have 29 letters from him; most of them are in his handwriting. I may have the last letter he wrote, He wrote it to me not many weeks before he died. In the following brother Hardeman eloquently compared two realms of learning and showed the beauty and blessings of the Holy Scriptures, and what he said further confirms why we need not expect anyone or any group to write a better book than the Bible!

"Take our manner of living, no longer is it characterized by the drudgery of the days to which our grandmothers belonged. Why some of you can perhaps remember when the wool from the backs of sheep was cut by hand clippers; that it was then combed and burred and trimmed, then carded into rolls, taken thence to the old spinning wheel. And then by physical foot power on the old loom woven into fabrics for the household. Then with a brass lamp and a yellow light, not bigger than your finger, with the eye of the needle in the wrong end, our grandmothers there sat and sewed and eked out a miserable existence for their families. All of that has not been so long past. But what about it now? Those days are gone forever, due to the progress of our modern civilization. That is but a sample of every phase and feature of things material with which you might have to do.

"But, friends, I want to ask of you: What progress has there been made in those more sacred and solemn and important relationships of man? What more do we know tonight about heaven, God, Christ, and the Holy Spirit, or the angelic host around the throne of God, than we did twenty centuries ago? Absolutely nothing! What do you know about God that you did not read from the Bible? What do you know about Christ other than the story penned by inspiration? What conception of heaven have you other than that gained from the Bible? What has all our education, our theories, our philosophies brought to us regarding the things that transcend the realms of time? Nothing! What do you know about man that was not known and written in that book called the Bible? What attribute or characteristic, passion, lust, appetite, desire, does he have – and what do you know about it – that is new to the Bible? Hear it! You know nothing! What do you know about sin that you did not learn from the book of God? What do you know about salvation outside of God's book? Not a thing! What progress has the human family made in analyzing our ownselves and figuring out a destiny that will bring to us the sweetest joys that earth can possibly have? Absolutely nothing. What commandment has ever been given since Christ and the apostles quit the walks of men? None. What promise is there after life's fitful fever is over that is not found in this blessed book? Not a single one.

"When you begin to study, therefore, the progress in the material world, from any point of consideration, it is marvelous to make comparison and the ratio is not a hundred nor a thousand, but thousandsfold of progress along every possible line of human thought and endeavor; but when you turn to those matters that outlive our existence here, and talk about the by and by, we have moved forward not one solitary hair's breadth. This suggests to us that the Bible comprehended and surveyed the whole field of human endeavor and our relationships one with another, and to our God, and pictured to us the golden glories of the eternal home beyond. There has been nothing added to what is found in the Bible." (*Hardeman's Tabernacle Sermons*, Vol. IV, pages 26, 27.)

"This second epistle, beloved, I now write unto you; in which I stir up your pure minds by way of remembrance: that ye may be mindful of the words which were spoken before by the holy prophets, and of the commandment of us the apostles of the Lord and Saviour...." (2 Peter 3:1,2.)

The apostles of Jesus Christ our Saviour were told by him, "Howbeit when he, the Spirit of truth, is come, he will guide you into all truth: for he shall not speak of himself; but whatsoever he shall hear, that shall he speak: and he will shew you things to come." (John 16:13.)

The "all truth" Jesus promised is in the New Testament which was written by men who were guided in what they wrote by the Lord.

Questions And Discussion Points

Let someone relate what the writer of the lesson said about his skeptic friend.

What was the skeptic's reply to the writer's proposal?

If the Bible is not God's word whose word is it?

Read Archibald Alexander's statement in the lesson. Discuss it.

Let the students state what they think are the most significant points in Alexander's statement.

What did Alexander say about the *Iliad* and *Paradise Lost*?

Discuss 2 Peter 3:1,2.

What did Jesus promise the apostles in John 16:13?

Chapter Fourteen

THE NEW TESTAMENT CANON

Remember, the word <u>canon</u> means a measuring cane or stick, and came to refer to what was measured. When something measures up to some standard, it is said to be canonized. The books of the Old Testament and the New Testament were written by men who were directed by the Spirit of God and there were many evidences that they were.

The word <u>canon</u> came to be used to refer to the books of the Bible, so they are called the Sacred Canon, or the Canon of Scripture.

"Let the word of Christ dwell in you richly in all wisdom; teaching and admonishing one another in psalms and hymns and spiritual songs, singing with grace in your hearts to the Lord." (Colossians 3:16.)

The Early Church

The Lord Jesus established his church on the first day of Pentecost following his resurrection and ascension. About three thousand people were added to the church that day by hearing the gospel, turning from their sins, confessing Christ, and being buried in baptism in order to get into Christ which is equated in the New Testament with getting into his body which is his church. (Read Acts 2.)

When the church was begun there was no book called the New Testament. Ten to fifteen years went by before the first book of the New Testament was written. Sixty to seventy years went by before all the books of the New Testament were written.

Before the first book of the New Testament was written, the Lord directed his church through preaching and teaching done by people he directed in the process we call inspiration.

Even after books of the New Testament began to be written, God taught and nourished the church through divinely guided teachers and preachers. (1 Corinthians 14.)

By the end of the first century all the books that are in our New Testament had been written. The final one of these books or divisions of the book we call the New Testament is the Book of Revelation.

Concerning the period and circumstances of which I have written above, an old friend and schoolmate of mine, Neil Lightfoot, wrote the following.

"When the church of Christ was first established it had no thought of a New Testament. Its Bible was the Old Testament and its new teachings were based on the authority of Christ as personally mediated through the apostles. Soon inspired men came to put in writing divine regulations directed both to churches and individuals. It was inevitable that these regulations would become normative, for Christians could not have less respect for them than for their Christ. Thus Paul's letters were carefully gathered into a single whole; next came a collection of the Four Gospels, and then all the others followed. Because these collections were made at different times and in various places, the contents of the collections were not always the same. This helps to explain why not all of the New Testament books were at first received without hesitation; while in other instances uncertainty of a books' authorship, as in the case of Hebrews, presented temporary obstacles to universal acceptance. This was the exception, however, rather than the rule; and gradually each book on its own merit – not without, Christians believe, a guiding Providence – took its place in the accepted canon of New Testament Scripture." (Neil Lightfoot, *How We Got The Bible*, Baker Book House, 1963, page 84.)

Remember, it was easy to identify one who wrote as he was directed by the Holy Ghost in the process we call inspiration. Those writers had credentials. They could work wonders or perform miracles. (2 Corinthians 12:12.) Gradually, therefore, as they wrote what we call the 27 books of the New Testament, these books were perceived by the early church to be the word of God.

The founder of Princeton Theological Seminary, Archibald Alexander stated the case well in the following statement.

"The slightest attention to the works of the Fathers, will convince anyone, that the writings of the apostles were held, from the beginning, in the highest estimation; that great pains were taken to distinguish the genuine productions of these inspired men, from all other books; that they were sought out with profound attention and veneration, not only in private, but publicly in the churches; and that they are cited and referred to, universally, as decisive on every point of doctrine, and as authoritative standards for the regulation of faith and practice." (Archibald Alexander, *The Canon Of The Old And New Testaments*, page 144.) "Fathers" in this statement refers to leading scholars in the church in the early centuries A.D.

Members of the church of Christ are not the only ones who accept just the 27 books of the New Testament Canon, or the books that ought to be in the New Testament. Protestants and Catholics (Roman and Greek) agree that the New Testament Canon consists of these 27 books. Liberal, and so-called Neo-Orthodox Protestants deny the full truthfulness of the 27 New Testament books, but this does not mean the books are not completely truthful and reliable.

"According as his divine power hath given unto us all things that pertain unto life and godliness, through the knowledge of him that hath called us to glory and virtue." (2 Peter 1:3.)

Archibald Alexander also presented a grand array of scholars of the early centuries A.D. who acknowledged the books of the New Testament. The following by him is a classic testimony regarding this enlightening and reassuring evidence.

"And here, as in the case of the Old Testament, we find, that at a very early period, catalogues of these books were published, by most of the distinguished Fathers whose writings have come down to us: the same has been done also, by several Councils, whose decrees are still extant.

"These catalogues, are, for the most part, perfectly harmonious. In a few of them, some books now in the Canon, are omitted, for which omission a satisfactory reason can commonly be assigned. In the first circulation of the Sacred Scriptures there was a great need of such lists; as the distant churches and common Christians, were liable to be imposed on by spurious writings, which seem to have abounded in those times. It was, therefore, a most important part of the instruction given to Christians, by their spiritual guides, to inform them accurately, what books belonged to the Canon. Great pains were taken, also, to know the truth on this subject. Pious bishops, for this single purpose, traveled into Judea, and remained there for some time, that they might learn accurately, every circumstance, relative to the authenticity of these writings.

"The first regular catalogue of the books of the New Testament, which we find on record, is by Origen, whose extensive Biblical knowledge highly qualified him to judge correctly in this case. He had not only read much, but traveled extensively, and resided a great part of his part of his life in the confines of Judea, in a situation favourable to accurate information, from every part of the church, where any of these books were originally published. Origen lived, and flourished, about one hundred years after the death of the Apostle John. He was, therefore, near enough to the time of the publication of these books, to obtain the most certain information of their authors. Most of the original writings of this great and learned man have perished, but his catalogue of the books of the New Testament has been preserved by Eusebius, in his *'Eccleciastical History.'* It was contained in Origen's *Homilies on the Gospel of Matthew*; and was repeated in his *Homilies on the Gospel of John.*

"In this catalogue, he mentions, the Four Gospels, the Acts of the Apostles, fourteen of the Epistles of Paul, two of Peter, three of John, and the book of Revelation. The enumeration includes all the present Canon, except the epistles of James, and Jude, but these were omitted by accident, not design; for in other parts of his writings, he acknowledges these Epistles as a part of the Canon. And while Origen furnishes us with so full a catalogue of the books now in the Canon, he inserts no others, which proves, that in his time, the Canon was well settled among the learned; and that the distinction between inspired writings and human compositions, was as clearly marked, as at any subsequent period." (*Canon Of Scripture*, pages 146, 147.)

The highly respected and classical set of volumes by Dr. John M'Clintock, and Dr. James Strong, entitled *Cyclopedia of Biblical, Theological and Ecclesiastical Literature*, contains much on the Canon of Scripture. Concerning the New Testament Canon they make the following points.

1. The Epistles of Paul were known by Peter. (2 Peter 3:15,16.)

2. Theophilus of Antioch of the second century wrote frequently of the New Testament writings.

3. Clement of Alexandria of the second and third centuries, frequently wrote about the New Testament Scriptures.

4. Tertullian of the second and third centuries, wrote of the New Testament in complete form.

5. Irenaeus was a disciple of Polycarp who was a disciple of the apostle John. Iranaeus repeatedly wrote about the writings of the New Testament as "the Holy Scriptures," and "the Oracles of God."

6. Origen the great Christian scholar of the second and third centuries and Eusebius of the third and fourth centuries, both enumerated the same New Testament books that we do.

The distinguished scholar Bruce Metzger of Princeton wrote considerably about the early Syriac Versions of the New Testament. He says five or six separate versions in Syriac were made during the first six centuries of the Christian era and that these are "noteworthy testimony to the vitality and scholarship of Syrian churchmen."

Dr. Metzger also says *Tatian's Diatessaron* was written about 170 A.D. which was a harmony of the four accounts of the life, death, and resurrection of Jesus of Nazareth by Matthew, Mark, Luke, and John.

According to Metzger, a scholar named Theophilus also wrote a harmony of Matthew, Mark, Luke and John in the second century. He adds that evidently throughout the first two centuries Christians in Antioch, Syria made use of the Old and New Testaments in Greek.

Dr. Metzger documents well what he says from ancient writings. See his book: *The Early Versions Of The New Testament*.

Questions And Discussion Points

1. Review the meaning of <u>canon</u> and the credentials of the Bible writers.

2. What should richly dwell in Christians according to Colossians 3:16?

3. Did Peter have a New Testament to preach from on Pentecost? Why?

4. Discuss what Neil Lightfoot said, which is recited in the lesson.

5. Discuss what Archibald Alexander said which is recited in the lesson.

6. Who were the Fathers referred to by Alexander?

7. Discuss who accepts the 27 books of the New Testament.

8. Where can we find all things that pertain to life and godliness referred to in 2 Peter 1:3?

Chapter Fifteen

OTHER EVIDENCES OF THE EARLY NEW TESTAMENT

In the previous chapter I presented some information regarding ancient translations of the New Testament to show that we now have the New Testament that people had in the early centuries A.D. There are other evidences which do the same.

Before his death, our Savior told his apostles, "I have yet many things to say unto you, but ye cannot bear them now. Howbeit when he, the Spirit of truth is come, he will guide you into all truth: for he shall not speak of himself; but whatsoever he shall hear, that shall he speak: and he will shew you things to come." (John 16:12,13.)

There are good evidences that we have the "all truth" of this promise in the New Testament. We should be grateful to all who have made it possible for us to have the book called the New Testament.

Writers Who Were Believers

There were believers in the second, third, and fourth centuries A.D. who quoted from the New Testament. Scholars say nearly all the New Testament has been found in these quotations. David Dalrymple said concerning his reading from the writings of believers of those early centuries, "I have found the entire New Testament except eleven verses." (Quoted by Charles Leach in: *Our Bible: How We Got It*, Moody Press, 1898, pages 35,36.)

Another report I read said all the New Testament has been found in those early writings by believers except seven verses.

Believers of the early centuries A.D. quoted from the New Testament just like many of us do. The New Testament was not only in existence in those early centuries, people believed for good reasons it was authoritative and that they should give careful attention to it!

Alexander Campbell said regarding the New Testament books, "There is not a writer on religion, which has come down to us from the second century (and of such writers the second century was not barren) who has not quoted these writings, less or more, as we do at the present day."

"But grow in grace, and in the knowledge of our Lord and Saviour Jesus Christ. To him be the glory both now and forever.

Amen." (2 Peter 3:18.) We can grow in this way because we have the wonderful book called the New Testament.

Nearly 6000 Ancient Greek Manuscripts

Scholars say nearly 6000 ancient Greek manuscripts of the New Testament scriptures have been found.

Not only are there many ancient Greek manuscripts of the New Testament, Dr. Berkley Micklesen says there are also thousands of old manuscripts in many other languages. These are classified in groups by Dr. Bruce Metzger of Princeton Theological Seminary in "The Evidence Of The Versions For The Text Of The New Testament," (*New Testament Manuscript Studies*, The University Of Chicago Press, 1950, pages 26,27.)

The original Greek manuscripts of the New Testament have not been found. However the thousands of manuscripts which have been found in so many places make it obvious that there were original manuscripts.

The nearly 6000 ancient Greek manuscripts of the New Testament are not all complete.

It is interesting that some translations of the New Testament books are older than the oldest Greek manuscripts of the New Testament that have been found. There is a small portion of the Book of John which is older than the well known oldest translations. This is a copy of John 18:31-33,37,38. Scholars say it had to have been written in the first half of the second century during the reign of the Roman Emperor Hadrian who reigned 118-138 A.D.

This small portion of John was found in 1920 by the famous Papyrologist, Dr. B. P. Grenfel. Later, C. H. Roberts made positive identification of it. This fragment is now in John Rylands Library in Manchester, England.

Chester Beatty, a British mining engineer obtained some Greek manuscripts of the New Testament in 1931 in Egypt which had allegedly been found in jars in an Egyptian graveyard. This significant find was announced November 17, 1931 by Sir Frederic Kenyon, Director of the British Museum in a news article. The finding of these manuscripts has been called "one of the most amazing discoveries in the twentieth century."

One of my old schoolmates, Dr. Neil Lightfoot says, "In addition to Mr. Beatty's collection, other parts of the same group were acquired by the University of Michigan and by private individuals. In all there are portions of twelve manuscripts. Nine of these contain parts of the Old Testament in Greek: considerable portions of Genesis, Numbers and Deuteronomy, and parts of Esther, Ezekiel, and Daniel. Three manuscripts in the group are of the New Testament books." (Neil R. Lightfoot, *How We Got The Bible*, Baker Book House, 1963, page 65.)

Scholars say these manuscripts were written in the early part of the third century A.D.

Dr. Henry Clarence Thiessen served as Chairman of the faculty of the Graduate School of Wheaton College in Wheaton, IL. In his excellent book, *Introduction To The New Testament* he presented a lengthy list of the names of scholars and "church fathers" of the second century A.D. and several centuries following who acknowledged the new Testament books as Holy Scripture. Some of them are as follows.

1. Ignatius, bishop of Antioch obviously was acquainted with what we call the New Testament. Dr. Thiessen says he was martyred about 116 A.D. *Webster's New Biographical Dictionary* says it was about 100 A.D. that he was arrested, taken to Rome and martyred by authority of Emperor Trajan.

2. Polycarp, bishop of Smyrna who lived 69 to 155 A.D. in his writings quoted a lot from many of the New Testament books.

3. Papias, bishop of Hierapolis who lived about 80 to 155 A.D. quoted much from the New Testament.

4. Melito, bishop of Sardis in the second century quoted from most of the books of the New Testament.

5. Epiphanius, bishop of Salamis and the island of Cyprus who lived about 315 to 403 made it obvious in his writings that he recognized the same New Testament books that we do.

6. Justin the Martyr lived about 100 to 165 A.D. He was a Greek born in Samaria. He wrote a number of books. Three of them are his *First Apology*, his *Second Apology*, and his *Dialogue With Trypho the Jew*. Justin traveled widely and finally settled in Rome where he founded a school. His writings were very important, and in them he quoted much from the New Testament.

As the New Testament church was falling away from the gospel just as Paul in the New Testament Scriptures prophesied it would, church leaders began to have Councils. Historical evidence shows that none of these Councils selected the books that should go into the New Testament Canon. The 27 books in our New Testaments, despite all rivals, were admitted into the Sacred Canon by their own obvious qualities and the overwhelming evidences that they were written by men who could prove by miracles that they were guided by Almighty God in what they wrote. Apparently, it was not until near the end of the fourth century that any Council even discussed the matter. Dr. Thiessen says the Council of Carthage in 397 released the first Counciliar decision on the New Testament. A prominent scholar and theologian named Augustine was one of the most influential members of this Council. One of the decisions that was made and announced about the New Testament by this Council demanded "that nothing be read in church under the title of Divine Scripture except the canonical books." This release or announcement also contained a list of the New Testament books that were held to be canonical and the list was exactly the same as our 27 books.

The Council of Carthage in 397 A.D. did not decide on and determine what the books of the New Testament ought to be. That had been decided centuries before, not by a human council, but by the worth and weight of the 27 books that were obviously divinely inspired writings.

The Roman Catholic Church tries to convince people that the Council of Carthage was a council of the Roman Catholic Church, and that it decided on what books should be in the New Testament, and therefore that we owe a great debt of gratitude to that church for giving us the New Testament. The Roman Catholic church did not even exist in 397 A.D. The church at that time was in the process of falling away as taught in 1 Timothy 4:1-6; 2 Timothy 4:1-6; and 2 Thessalonians chapter two. In 397 A.D. there was no universal earthly head of the apostate church called "pope." The first universal "Pope" was Boniface III, Patriarch of Rome and became recognized as "Pope" in 606 A.D.

The Roman Catholic Church did not give us the New Testament. The New Testament was in the world long before that church existed. The church of Christ about which we read in the New Testament, and of which I am a member, did not give us that book. God the Father through the agency of the Holy Ghost gave us the New Testament and also the Old Testament as he directed writers of the Bible by inspiration.

Lectionaries

Beginning in the sixth century A.D. reading lessons of New Testament scriptures were used in the public church services. Substantial portions of these scriptures were in each reading lesson. These were called lectionaries. More than 1600 of these have been found and classified. They constitute great evidence not only that the New Testament existed, but also was read and studied in church services.

Concerning the law of God under which he lived, David said to his God, "O how love I thy law! It is my meditation all the day." (Psalm 119:97.) Christians should say the same regarding the New Testament scriptures.

The following is from the Introductory Essay by John Stoughton in *Matthew Henry's Bible Commentary*, Volume I (of six volumes) MSS is an abbreviation of "manuscripts."

"The second inquiry, touching the genuineness of our present text, also requires some notice. It has been alleged, by the enemies of Christianity, that the text of the New Testament has been greatly altered at different times. Mr. Taylor, in his *Manifesto*, published some years since, stated, that Christian emperors, bishops, and councils, issued, from time to time, formal acts and edicts for the general alteration of the Scriptures. Now, a more shameless falsehood could not be uttered. There is no evidence whatever of any such edicts. And, moreover, such an alteration of the MSS, as he asserts took place, is in itself an impossibility. Various MSS, of the New Testament existed at that time; and it was utterly beyond the power of any man, or any number of men, to collect all these copies together, and to alter them. 'The tyranny of such attempts,' observes Dr. Pye Smith, 'make men indignant; and when the effectual concealment of a thing so small as a few rolls or leaves of parchment was so very easy, they would not tamely part with a valuable possession, in many cases a family inheritance, or the property of a society.' In further refutation of the absurd notion of a corruption of MSS, we may refer to a passage in Augustine, a writer of the fifth century; who, in reply to the calumny of the Manicheans, that their opponents falsified the Scriptures – reminds them, 'that whoever had first attempted such a corruption of the sacred books, would have immediately been confuted by a multitude of ancient MSS, which were in the hands of all Christians.'"

The following from the same essay by Mr. Stoughton is a clever and clear refutation of some false claims about the Bible.

"Rival sects have appealed to Scriptures in support of their respective dogmas, and have been equally jealous of any tampering with the avowed standard of their faith. Even had they been disposed to corrupt the Word of God, they would have acted as a check on each other, sufficiently powerful to prevent their carrying their wishes into effect. Moreover, the large body of quotations, already noticed, to be found in early Christian authors, and the numerous ancient versions which are extant, supply evidence in favour of the genuineness of our present text, as strong as that which they supply in favour of its antiquity. But it has been asserted by those who disbelieve in Christianity, that learned Christian critics and divines do themselves admit that the Scriptures have undergone alterations from time to time. Witness, they say, the various readings of the text, which have been collected by learned men. By various readings, are meant those differences in words or sentences which we find in the MSS of the same book. Now these differences have been collected, to the amount of many thousands. But what, after all, is the extent of these differences? Very little indeed. They are almost all very slight and immaterial variations; such as relate to the spelling or the position of a word, the employment of a particular term, or a synonyme, or the punctuation of a sentence. Very few, indeed, produce any alteration in the meaning; and where they do produce any such alteration, they are not sufficient to disturb our faith in a single article of the Christian system, because each doctrine is supported by passages, about the perfect genuineness of which there is not dispute. The truth is, that an examination of the subject confirms the genuineness of the sacred books. MSS, found in all parts of the world, and written at different times, are subjected to the most minute critical investigation; and except in the trifling matters just noticed, they are found to agree: they all exhibit, substantially, the same text; no differences are found, but those which time and other circumstances must have produced without a standing miracle to prevent them. Is not this convincing evidence of the genuineness of the records? What has been thrown in our teeth, as an objection is, in fact, a most overwhelming argument in our favour. The enemies of Christianity forget themselves in appealing to it. They handle a weapon which wounds and destroys their own cause. It is like the sword of Goliath, which after being waved in proud deviance before the armies of the living God, becomes the means of slaying the very foe who wielded it."

No date of publication is on the title page of the edition of Mr. Henry's commentary in which is Mr. Stoughton's essay. Matthew Henry was born in Wales October 18, 1662, and he died in 1714. Apparently this edition of his commentary was published quite some time after his death. On the title page it is called *"A New And Illustrated Edition."* Whatever the date it was published, it was a long time ago, because in the following portion of his essay, Mr. Stoughton refers to "five hundred, at least" of ancient Greek manuscripts of the New Testament had been found. Now approximately 6000 have been found.

"Some classical productions rest on the authority of one or two MSS. Even our editions of Herodotus are taken from an examination of not more than fifteen MSS,. and those of no higher antiquity than the fifteenth century. But five hundred, at least, have been collected for our New Testament, and many of these of a very early date; some as old as the fifth or fourth century. The veneration of Christians for their sacred books, their diligence in copying them, their jealousy of interpolations, the large body of quotations from these books in other writings still extant, and the versions made at an early period, are all points of evidence in support of the genuineness of the New Testament, incomparably more strong then can be supplied in favour of any volume in profane literature."

In the following from Mr. Stoughton's essay, he refers to Philo and Josephus who were Jewish historians who lived while Jesus Christ was on earth.

"Our remarks have related to the literary history of the New Testament. That the Old Testament existed in the time of Jesus, and long before, is apparent from what is said of it in the New; and, therefore, the antiquity of the latter is a proof of the still higher antiquity of the former. Philo and Josephus supply proofs to the same effect; and the Septuagint is monument of the existence of the Hebrew Scriptures then. Thence we are carried back to prior ages; and it is perfectly impossible, with any show of reason, to account for their origin at all, unless we assign to them those dates which, in all ages, have been given them by the Jewish people. Some parts of the Old Testament are, unquestionably, the oldest literary remains in the world.

"Of the careful preservation of the Hebrew text for the last thirteen hundred years, we have a proof in the labours of the Jews to secure the greatest accuracy. Owing to such labours, comparatively few various readings are to be found in their MSS. of any importance. Though in themselves numerous, they for the most part relate to matters utterly insignificant, such as the omission of a letter in a word. Learned men acknowledge that the collation of them hardly repays the labour bestowed on it, though, indeed, it is highly gratifying to possess such evidence of the genuineness of the text."

Questions And Discussion Points

1. What did Jesus tell his apostles about all truth?

2. How much of the New Testament did David Dalrymple say he found in the writings of early centuries A.D.?

3. What did Alexander Campbell say about writers on religion from the second century A.D. until his time?

4. How many ancient Greek manuscripts of the New Testament have been found?

5. Are there any known ancient manuscripts of the New Testament in languages other than Greek?

6. Are all translations of the New Testament newer than the oldest Greek manuscripts of it?

7. What are the Chester Beatty manuscripts?

8. Discuss Lectionaries.

Chapter Sixteen

ANCIENT INFIDELS HELP!

"Heaven and earth shall pass away, but my words shall not pass away." (Matthew 24:36.)

"For all flesh is as grass, and all the glory of man as the flower of the grass. The grass withereth, and the flower thereof falleth away: but the word of the Lord endureth forever. And this is the word which by the gospel is preached unto you." (1 Peter 1:24,25.)

Some ask, "How can we be assured that the books in our New Testament are what were in the New Testament soon after the apostles had all died?" Anyone willing to study and really look into this matter will surely be completely convinced that the books in our New Testament are the same ones which people of the first and second centuries A.D. had.

Infidels Are Good Evidence!

Scholars have long known that infidels of the first three or four centuries showed in their writings that they were familiar with the New Testament writings. They not only wrote profusely concerning matters recorded in the New Testament, they also quoted from it frequently.

In his debate with the atheist Robert Owen in 1829 in Cincinnati, Ohio, Alexander Campbell said that the Epicurean philosopher Celsus who was also an infidel and lived in the second century A.D. showed great familiarity with the New Testament Scriptures. Celsus had a correspondence debate with the great Christian scholar named Origen. Campbell said in his debate with Owen that Origen said Celsus gave about 80 quotations from the New Testament in some of his writings. I have an 1852 edition of the Campbell-Owen Debate, and this is stated on page 278.

Alexander Campbell wrote a book entitled *The Christian Preacher's Companion, Or The Gospel Facts Sustained By The Testimony Of Unbelieving Jews And Pagans*. In it he recited from infidels of the first two or three centuries A.D. the evidences of their familiarity with the New Testament Scriptures. These infidels quoted from, and wrote about things in the New Testament to try to get around what it said. But this proves the New Testament scriptures existed when they lived! And it proves those New Testament scriptures were well recognized as authoritative!

Campbell said the following concerning this matter on pages 154,155, 156 in the book cited above.

"It is no mean tribute to the fidelity and credibility of the authors of the New Testament, that if their work were now extinct, and we were thrown upon the records of unbelieving Jews and pagans, we could make out substantially the same narrative of all the leading gospel facts and events found in the New Testament. And still more gratifying, were we compelled to publish in one volume everything found in the first two centuries, when all things were comparatively fresh, touching the Christian institution, we could not find one authenticated fact that would militate against us, or impair the full strength of any one fact or event recorded in the Christian scriptures."

After listing the names of many of the infidels and pagans about whom he wrote in the book cited above, Campbell then said the following could be ascertained from their writings.

1. That the Jews' religion preceded the Christian, is of the highest antiquity, and distinguished by peculiarities the most extraordinary from every other ancient or modern religion.

2. That John the Baptist appeared in Judea, in the reign of Herod the Great, a reformer and a preacher of singular pretensions, of great sanctity of life, and was well received by the people; but was cruelly and unjustly murdered in prison by Herod the Tetrarch.

3. That Jesus, who is called the Messiah, was born in Judea, in the reign of Augustus Caesar, of a very humble and obscure woman, and amidst a variety of extraordinary circumstances.

4. That he was, while an infant, on account of persecution, carried into Egypt, but was brought back again into the country of his nativity.

5. That there were certain prophetic writings of high antiquity, from which it had been inferred that a very extraordinary personage was to arise in Judea, or in the East, and from thence to carry his conquests over the whole earth.

6. That this person was generally expected all over the East about the time in which the gospel began to be preached.

7. That Jesus, who is called Christ, taught a new and strange doctrine.

8. That by some means he performed certain wonderful and supernatural actions in confirmation of his new doctrine.

9. That he collected disciples in Judea, who, though of humble

birth and very low circumstances, became famous through various parts of the Roman Empire, in consequence of the progress of the Christian doctrine.

10. That Jesus Christ was the founder of a new religion, now called the Christian religion.

11. That while Pontius Pilate was governor in Judea, and Tiberius emperor in Rome, he was publicly executed as a criminal.

12. That this new religion was then checked for a while.

13. That, by some strange occurrence not mentioned, it broke out again and progressed with the most astonishing rapidity.

14. That in the days of Tacitus there was in the city of Rome an immense number of Christians.

15. That these Christians were, during the reign of Nero, or about thirty years after the death of Christ, persecuted to death by that emperor.

16. That constancy (called obstinacy by some pagan governors) in maintaining the heavenly and exclusively divine origin of their religion, is the only crime proved against the Christians, as appears from all the records of their enemies, on account of which they suffered death.

17. That in the year 70, or before, those who had seen Jesus Christ had died, Jerusalem and the Temple were destroyed by the Romans, and all the tremendous calamities foretold of that time by Moses and Christ were fully visited upon that disobedient and gainsaying people.

18. That the Christians were people who had made a confession of their faith, and were baptized, and met at stated times to worship the Lord.

19. That in their stated meetings they bound themselves, by the solemnities of their religion, to abstain from all moral evil, and to practice all moral good.

20. That the communities which they established were well organized, and were under the superintendence of bishops and deacons.

21. That Jews, Gentiles, barbarians, of all castes, and persons of every rank and condition of life, at the risk and sacrifice of the friendship of the world, or property, and of life, embraced this religion and conformed to all its moral and religious requisitions.

What brother Campbell presented from the writings of ancient infidels is that even though they tried to destroy the Christian teachings and the Christian religion they were actually helping it without realizing it!

"Therefore we ought to give the more earnest heed to the things which we have heard, lest at any time we should let them slip." (Hebrews 2:1.)

Another Splendid Source That Affirms How Infidels Helped

The distinguished Bible scholar S. S. Schmucker published a two volume set of books entitled *Biblical Theology*. My copy of Volume 1 was published in 1826. Schmucker's works are translations of writings of two German scholars, Dr. Theophilus Christian Storr, and Dr. C. C. Flatt. Dr. Storr was a professor of theology in the University of Tübingen.

Professor Schumacker said of Professor Storr in his Preface, "His numerous philological and exegetical works rank among the first critical productions of Germany, and few men have attained such profundity or erudition, and at the same time preserved so humble and faithful an adherence to the doctrines of the Bible, as are displayed in the literary and theological career of Dr. Storr."

Professor Schumacker said Dr. Flatt was in no way inferior to Dr. Storr. Of both of them he wrote, "These distinguished champions of the truth sustained the cause of orthodoxy for upward of twenty years, and published from time to time, the most able replies to the several systems of infidelity which sprung up in Europe. Having been harassed by metaphysical and speculative and infidel systems of pretended Christianity, they were taught the absolute necessity of building their faith exclusively on the word of God; and the present work is purely of this Biblical character. It is confined to the doctrines which are taught in the sacred volume."

Drs. Storr and Flatt present a splendid array of documented evidence that infidels of the first three or four centuries A. D. vainly attempted in their writings to disprove the books of the New Testament. These infidels included Celsus, Porphyry, and others.

Following their presentation of what the infidels wrote about the New Testament books, Storr and Flatt wrote, "There is nothing strange in the preceding heathen testimony in favour of the Christian Scriptures. Nor is it by any means surprising that pagan writers should be acquainted with the facts, established by their testimony in the preceding illustrations, when we recollect what Tertullian says to them in his defense of the Christians against the heathen...." (page 22.)

Questions And Discussion Points

1. Discuss Matthew 24:36 and 1 Peter 1:24,25.

2. What question do some ask about the books in the New Testament?

3. Who was Robert Owen and whom did he debate?

4. How did infidels of the early centuries A.D. help us concerning the New Testament canon?

5. Discuss things from the New Testament that have been found in the writings of those early infidels.

6. What did those infidels say about confession of faith and baptism?

7. What did those infidels say about bishops and deacons?

8. What did those infidels say about the convictions and morality of early Christians?

Chapter Seventeen

WE CANNOT COMPREHEND
THE PROCESS OF INSPIRATION

Even though it is reasonable to believe the Bible was written by men whom God directed by His Spirit, we cannot comprehend this great work of the Spirit of God.

"If there be a God, an all-wise mind or spirit by whom all things were created; and if man have mind or spirit, it is not impossible for that great and glorious being to reveal Himself and His will to man. Our inability to describe or conceive of the manner in which this is done is no just argument against it, for that action of the Spirit of God upon the mind of man, which is denoted by the word inspiration, is not more inconceivable than the ordinary action of the human mind upon the body; and if everything be banished from the world which we cannot comprehend, there will be little or nothing left." (James Smith, *The Christian's Defence*, page 23.)

Dr. Smith's reference to "the ordinary action of the human mind upon the body" is indeed thought provoking. I certainly am not capable of explaining how God Almighty worked on men to enable them to write the Bible, and I do not believe anyone else can do this. Many evidences make it easy to believe that God did this. It is easier to believe he did this than it is to believe he did not do it. Those who contend he did not do it, need to think about many things, none of which they can explain, but none of which they deny.

The ordinary action of the human mind upon the human body in which it dwells presupposes the existence of the human mind and the human body. Perhaps to a great extent both the mind and the body are taken for granted by most people.

A part of the human body is its brain, but the brain is not the mind. The mind dwells in the brain. The mind is one thing; the brain is something else. The physical or cellular structure of the brain is the same after a person dies as it was before he died. Scientists struggle in dealing with the question concerning the differences in the mind and the brain. After a person dies his brain is still in his body, but his mind is no longer in his brain. We can explain how the mind can dwell in the brain while one is living, but not after he dies.

The human mind cannot fully comprehend itself or its dwelling place the human brain. Here is a statement that is a sample of the evidence for this awesome fact.

"The human brain, which weighs about 1,400 grams (3 pounds), has the consistency of semi-soft cheese. Like the spinal cord, the brain is made up of both 'white matter' – the fiber tracts – and gray matter. The gray matter consists of nerve cell bodies and glial (glue) cells, which apparently support and nourish the neurons. The glial cells may also play a role in ironic balance and thus in electric potentials. In some areas of the brain, neurons and glial cells are so densely packed that a single cubic centimeter of gray matter contains some six million cell bodies, with each neuron connected to as many as 80,000 others.

"For at least 2,000 years, people have wondered about the relationship between the brain – this mass of semisoft substance – and the mind, the center of consciousness, thought, and emotion." (*Biology*, by Helena Curtis, Worth Publishers, Inc., Second Printing, August 1979, page 753.)

Another source says the human brain contains about 10 billion nerve cells, and that on the average, each of the 10 billion is connected with about 1,000 others. (*Integrated Principles of Zoology*, by Cleveland Hickman, Larry Roberts, and Frances Hickman, Seventh Edition, Times Mirror/Mosby College Publishing, 1984, page 769.)

The foregoing comments constitute a very minute description of the awesome complexity and structure of the human brain. It and the human mind that dwells in it certainly should be overwhelming evidence of our Creator God. How the human mind operates on the highly complex human body is just as difficult to grasp as the operation of the one who obviously created human bodies and human minds on the human minds of those approximately 40 men who wrote the Bible! Indeed, "All Scripture is given by inspiration of God, and is profitable for doctrine, for reproof, for correction, for instruction in righteousness, that the man of God may be complete, thoroughly equipped for every good work." (2 Timothy 3:16,17.)

While we cannot comprehend the process of divine inspiration, and how the mind of God worked on the minds of the men who wrote the Bible enabling them to write that sacred volume, we should be very concerned about what God said to us through those men.

Belshazzar the king of Babylon made a great feast to a thousand of his lords. He commanded that the sacred vessels his father

Nebuchadnezzar had stolen from the house of God in Jerusalem be brought so he, his wives, his concubines, and his princes could drink wine from them at the great feast. As they were drinking, fingers of a man's hand wrote on the plaster of the wall of Belshazzar's palace. When he saw the part of the hand that wrote, his countenance was changed, and his mind was burdened, and his hip joints were loosed and his knees smote each other! (Daniel 5.)

There is no indication that Belshazzar appointed an investigative committee to try to find out how part of a man's hand could write on the wall, but instead, "The king cried aloud to bring the astrologers, the Chaldeans, and the soothsayers" (Daniel 5:7) in order to learn what it was that the fingers wrote on the wall and the interpretation or meaning of it. They could not tell the king what the writing was, and what it meant, but Daniel the prophet of God told him.

Daniel preached a strong sermon to Belshazzar and at the end of it he told him the writing was Mene, Mene, Tekel, Upharsin, and it meant God had numbered his kingdom and finished it, and that Belshazzar was weighed in the balance and found wanting, and that his kingdom was divided and given to the Medes and Persians.

In that night Belshazzar was killed and Darius the Mede took his kingdom.

Just as Belshazzar was concerned about what those fingers wrote instead of about how such could be done, even so, we should be greatly concerned about what God tells us in the Book which was written by men whom he guided, instead of feeling that we are obligated to comprehend the process of God's Spirit guiding them. God's Spirit gave them the words they wrote, but we cannot comprehend the process by which he did it. We can study what God's will is for us. The reason for doing this is stressed in many passages of the Bible. Some of them follow.

"Every word of God is pure: he is a shield unto them that put their trust in him." (Proverbs 30:5.)

"The words of the Lord are pure words: as silver tried in a furnace of earth, purified seven times." (Psalm 12:6.)

"Wherefore lay apart all filthiness and superfluity of naughtiness, and receive with meekness the engrafted word which is able to save your souls." (James 1:21.)

Gaussen Stressed The Point

Some scholars consider a book by S. R. L. Gaussen on the inspiration of the Bible as the best on the subject. I own a copy of his book which was published in 1850. It was translated from French into English by Edward Norris Kirk. Gaussen was a professor of theology in Geneva, Switzerland. His book is entitled: *Theopneusty, Or The Plenary Inspiration Of The Holy Scriptures*.

Professor Gaussen wrote considerably in this book about the matter of our not understanding how the Spirit of God worked through men so they could write the Bible. He also stressed the importance of our recognizing the Bible as being truly God's word. The following are samples of what he wrote on this.

"At the same time, it should be distinctly observed, that this miraculous operation of the Holy Spirit had not for its object the sacred writers, who were only his instruments, and who were soon to pass away; but its object was the sacred books themselves, which were destined to reveal to the church from age to age, the immutable counsels of God.

"The influence which was exercised upon these men, and of which they themselves were conscious in very different degrees has never been defined to us. Nothing authorizes us to explain it. The Scriptures themselves have never presented to us its mode or its measure as an object of study. They speak of it always incidentally, they never connect our piety with it. That alone which they propose as the object of our faith is the inspiration of their word; is the divinity of their books; between these they make no difference. Their word, say they, is theopneustic; their books are of God, whether they recount mysteries or a past anterior to the creation, or those of a future posterior to the return of the Son of Man; the eternal counsels of the most High, the secrets of the human heart, or the deep things of God; whether they give utterance to their own emotions or record their own recollections, relate contemporaneous events, copy genealogies or make extracts from inspired documents; their writings are inspired; their statements are directed by heaven; it is always God who speaks, who relates, ordains or reveals by their mouth, and who, to accomplish it, employs their personality in different degrees. For 'the Spirit of the Lord was upon them, and his word upon their tongue.' And if it is always the word of man, because it is always men who utter it, it is likewise always the word of God, for it is always

God that superintends, guides and employs them. They give their narrations, their doctrines, or their precepts, 'not in the words which man's wisdom teacheth, but which the Holy Spirit teacheth.' And it is thus that God has constituted himself not only the voucher of all these facts, the author of all these ordinances, and the revealer of all these truths, but that also he has caused them to be given to the Church in the precise order, measure and terms which he has judged most conducive to his heavenly design.

"If then, we are asked how this theopneustic work was accomplished in the men of God, we should reply, that we do not know.

"Such is the fact of Theopneusty; the divine power in causing the Holy Scriptures to be written by inspired men, has, almost uniformly put in operation their understandings, their wills, their memories and all their individualities (as we shall presently shew).

"It is thus that God, who would make known to his elect, in an eternal book, the spiritual principles of the divine philosophy; has dictated its pages, during sixteen centuries, to priests, kings, warriors, shepherds, tax-gatherers, fishermen, scribes, and tent-makers. Its first line, its last line, all its instructions, understood or not understood, are from the same author; and this is sufficient for us. Whoever the writers may have been, and whatever their circumstances, their impressions, or their understanding of the book; they have all written with a faithful, superintended hand, on the same scroll, under the dictation of the same Master, to whom a thousand years are as one day; such is the origin of the Bible. I will not waste my time in vain questions; I will study the book. It is the word of Moses, the word of Amos, the word of John, the word of Paul; but it is the mind of God and the word of God." (Pages 34, 35, 41.)

Questions And Discussion Points

Let someone read what James Smith said.

Can we comprehend the process of how God guided the writers of the Bible?

Let someone relate the story of Belshazzar. What does it illustrate relative to the subject of the lesson.

Read and discuss the scriptures quoted in the lesson?

Who was S. R. L. Gaussen?

What is the title of the book he wrote from which he is quoted in the lesson?

Name things Gaussen stressed in the quotations from his book.

Have you ever read a book on the inspiration of the Bible?

Chapter Eighteen

THE GOD BREATHED SCRIPTURES

"All scripture is given by inspiration of God, and is profitable for doctrine, for reproof, for correction, for instruction in righteousness: that the man of God may be perfect, thoroughly furnished unto all good works." (2 Timothy 3:16,17.)

The word inspiration in this text is a translation of Greek theopneustos, which means God breathed. The word inspiration came from two Latin words: in and spiare. Spiare means to breathe. So, the word inspiration literally means to breathe in, whereas theopneustos means God breathed. God did not breathe in, when giving his word, but he breathed out. The word expiration expresses this concept. When we use the word inspiration referring to the scriptures we need to mean that God breathed out his word. The word pneustos in theopneustos means wind, breath, or spirit.

The scriptures were breathed out by God. In using the Greek word theopneustos in 2 Timothy 3:16, Paul was saying the Scriptures he referred to were of divine origin. He doubtless referred to the Old Testament Scriptures and any New Testament Scriptures which were then available.

Paul said of his own writings that he was writing what the Holy Spirit said. (1 Timothy 4:1.)

The scriptures did not come into being by the minds of men that were not guided by God. The scriptures were breathed out by God. Of course this is a figure of speech designed to convey the idea that the scriptures in the Bible were written by those whom God guided.

Inspiration of the Bible means there was miraculous action of the Spirit of God upon the minds of those who wrote the Bible that caused them to write only as God willed!

Gaussen On Theopneusty

Professor Gaussen, who is quoted in the previous chapter, wrote some splendid statements on theopneusty, or the God-breathing of the Holy Scriptures. The following is an example.

"In theory, we might say that a religion could be divine, without the miraculous inspiration of its books. It might be possible, for example, to conceive of a Christianity without Theopneusty; and it might perhaps, be conceived that every other miracle of our religion, except that, was a fact. In this supposition, (which is totally unauthorized) the eternal Father would have given his Son to the world; the all-creating Word, made flesh, would have undergone the death of the cross for us, and have sent down upon the apostles the spirit of wisdom and miraculous powers; but, all these mysteries of redemption once accomplished, he would have abandoned to these men of God the work of writing our sacred books, according to their own wisdom; and their writings would have presented to us only the natural language of their supernatural illuminations, of their convictions and their charity. Such an order of things is undoubtedly a vain supposition, directly contrary to the testimony of the Scriptures as to their own nature; but, without remarking here, that it explains nothing; and that, miracle for miracle, that of illumination is not less inexplicable than Theopneusty; without further saying that the word of God possesses a divine power peculiar to itself: such an order of things, if it were realized, would have exposed us to innumerable errors, and plunged us into the most ruinous uncertainity."

Then Professor Gaussen wrote that if the writers of the Bible had not been divinely guided in what they wrote, their writings would have been given less authority than is granted to the writings of Augustine, Bernard, Luther, Calvin and a multitude of others like them. Concerning these writers he said the following.

"We are sufficiently aware how many imprudent words and erroneous propositions mar the most beautiful pages of these admirable writers. And yet the apostles (on the supposition we have just made), would have been subjected still more than they, to serious errors; since they could not have had, like the doctors of the church, the word of God, by which to correct their writings; and since they would have been compelled to invent the entire language of religious science; for a science, we know, is more than half formed, when its language is made. What fatal errors, what grievous ignorance, what inevitable imprudence had necessarily accompanied, in them, a revelation without Theopneusty; and in what deplorable doubts had the church then been left! Errors in the selection of facts, errors in estimating them, errors in stating them, errors in the conception of the relations which they hold to doctrines, errors in the expression of these doctrines themselves, errors of omission, errors of language, errors of exaggeration, errors in the adoption of national, provincial or party prejudices, errors in the anticipations of the future and in the estimate of the past."

Comparing such a record of errors as would have been produced by uninspired men, Gaussen then wrote:

"But, thanks to God, it is not so with our sacred books. They contain no errors; all their writings are inspired of God. 'Holy men of God spake as they were moved by the Holy Ghost; not in the words which man's wisdom teacheth, but which the Holy Ghost teacheth'; so that none of these words ought to be neglected, and we are called to respect them and to study them even to their least iota and to their least tittle, for these 'words of the Lord are pure words; as silver tried in a furnace of earth, they are perfect.' These assertions, themselves testimonies of the word of God, contain precisely our last definition of Theopneusty, and lead us to characterize it finally, as 'that inexplicable power which the Divine Spirit formerly exercised over the authors of the Holy Scriptures, to guide them even in the employment of the words they were to use, and to preserve them from all error, as well as from every omission.'"

Inspiration And Revelation

That which enabled the writers of the Bible to write that blessed Book, which we call inspiration, was revelation from Almighty God, but not all revelation is inspiration. Archibald Alexander, the distinguished scholar, and founder of Princeton Theological Seminary wrote the following on this.

"There is also a difference between inspiration and revelation. All revelations are not made by a suggestion of truth to the mind of an individual. God often spake to people of old by audible voices, and communicated his will by the mission of angels. Many persons have thus received divine revelations, who had no pretensions to inspiration. All the people of Israel who stood before God at Mount Sinai, heard his voice uttering the Ten Commandments, and yet no one would say that all these were inspired. So also when Christ was upon earth, in more instances than one, a voice was heard declaring that he was the beloved Son of God. Indeed, all who had the opportunity of hearing Christ's discourses might be said to receive a revelation immediately from God; but it would be absurd to say that all these were inspired. Dr. Dick is of opinion, that the word revelation would be more expressive, as being more comprehensive, than suggestion, which last conveys the idea of an operation of the mind; whereas, truth, in many cases, was made known in other ways. But for the reason stated above, it would not do to substitute the word revelation for inspiration; inasmuch as multitudes received revelations who had no claim to inspiration. And when inspiration is confined to those who wrote the books of Scriptures, no other word would so clearly express the idea." (*Alexander's Evidences of Christianity*, page 224.)

In one of the classes I attended which N. B. Hardeman taught at Freed-Hardeman College over 50 years ago, we studied a book entitled, *Evidences Of Christianity* by the distinguished Christian scholar, J. W. McGarvey which was published in 1886 by Standard Publishing Company in Cincinnati, Ohio. It is two volumes in one. Like all of brother McGarvey's many books it is a classic work.

On pages 200 and 201 of the second volume McGarvey gave a summary of the evidences he had presented which strongly support the claim that the New Testament Scriptures were indeed God breathed or were written by men who were inspired of God!

Here is brother McGarvey's summary.

"1. The promise of the Holy Spirit to abide permanently in the Apostles with miraculous power was made by Jesus, and it was realized in the experience of the Twelve from and after the first Pentecost following the resurrection. The Spirit was also from time to time and in divers places imparted by the Apostles to other faithful persons. This was their inspiration.

"2. The Spirit thus abiding in the inspired, brought to their remembrance, to the full extent that was needful, the words and acts of Jesus. It guaranteed, therefore, a record of these words and acts, precisely such as God willed.

"3. It brought to the inspired persons revelations concerning the past, the present and the future; and when occasion required, it revealed to them the secret thoughts of living men. For this reason we can rely implicitly on the correctness of every thought which these men have expressed on these subjects.

"4. The Spirit within them taught them how to speak the things thus revealed, by teaching to the full extent needed the words in which to express them; yet, in quoting others, not always the exact words; and it demonstrated this fact to lookers-on by causing the inspired at times to speak in tongues which they had never learned, but which were known to those who heard. This affords a perfect guarantee that these revelations were really made, and that they are expressed in the most suitable words.

"5. By thus acting within and through the inspired men, the Spirit enabled them to speak on all occasions, even when life was at stake, without anxiety as to how or what they should say, and to speak with consummate wisdom, yet without premeditation. It brought about the fact expressed in the Hebraistic formula: 'It is not ye that speak, but the Spirit of your Father that speaketh in you.'

"6. The Spirit enabled the inspired on all suitable occasions to demonstrate the presence of its power within them, by manifestations of it in the way of physical 'powers, signs and wonders' – a demonstration which the human mind has ever demanded of men claiming to bear messages from God.

"7. From the fact that these men spoke and wrote as the Spirit willed, it follows that what they wrote out of their own personal experience and observation, as well as that which was revealed to them, has the Spirit's approval as a part of the record."

I do not know who wrote the following, but I know it is a classic summary of what the Bible is. It supports strongly the claim the Holy Scriptures were indeed God breathed.

Concerning the Bible someone wrote the following. "This Book Contains: The mind of God, the state of man, the doom of sinners, the way of salvation and the happiness of the faithful. Its doctrine is holy, its precepts are binding, its histories are true and its decisions immutable. Read it to be wise, believe it to be safe, practice it to be holy. It is light to guide you, food to support you, and comfort to cheer you. It is the traveler's map, the pilgrim's staff, the pilot's compass, the Christian's charter. Here paradise is restored, heaven opened and the gates of hell disclosed. Christ is its supreme subject, our good its design, and the glory of God its end. It should fill the memory, rule the heart and guide the feet. Read it slowly, frequently and prayerfully. It is a mine of wealth, a paradise of glory and a river of pleasure. It is given in life, will be opened after death, executed in judgment and shall stand forever. It involves the highest responsibility, rewards all righteous labor and condemns all who trifle with its holy contents."

Questions And Discussion Points

Have each one to memorize 2 Timothy 3:16,17.

What does inspiration mean? Discuss.

Read and discuss what professor Gaussen said in the lesson.

Was all revelation inspiration? Discuss.

Do you take the Bible seriously to show you believe it came from God?

Do you study the Bible enough to show you believe it came from God?

Do you have any tools to help you in the Bible study? Some are a Bible dictionary and a concordance.

Will you resolve to spend more time studying the Bible?

Chapter Nineteen

DID GOD GIVE THEM THE THOUGHTS OR THE WORDS?

Some have said God just gave the writers of the Bible thoughts and allowed them to express these thoughts in their own words in the Bible. If this is true, what assurance do we have that the writers expressed those thoughts correctly?

Writers Did Not Always Understand

The Spirit of God gave the Bible writers the very words which they gave to us in the original manuscripts of the Bible. One proof of this is the fact that the writers did not always understand the words of messages which God gave through them. The following are some examples.

1. "And I heard, but understood not: then said I, O my Lord, what shall be the end of these things? And he said, Go thy way, Daniel: for the words are closed up and sealed till the time of the end." (Daniel 12:8,9.)

In previous verses Daniel recorded things God revealed to him. These are things he did not understand even though he wrote them. In the rest of that last chapter of Daniel, he recorded things God said to him. It is doubtful he understood them, but God assured him the things would come to pass.

The fact that Bible writers did not always understand their own writings does not reflect on their being inspired, but rather shows they were directed by the Almighty!

2. "For verily I say unto you, that many prophets and righteous men have desired to see those things which ye see, and have not seen them; and to hear those things which ye hear and have not heard them." (Matthew 13:17.)

Jesus had just recited words by Isaiah (Esaias) the Old Testament prophet and said what Isaiah prophesied was fulfilled in the attitudes of some who lived when Jesus was speaking. Isaiah prophesied much concerning the coming of Jesus the Messiah and the Messanic kingdom. He was one of those included in the "many prophets and righteous men" who desired to know the meaning of what they foretold but did not know. This proves they were not given thoughts by

God to express in their own words, but they were given the very words by God which he wanted them to speak and write whether they understood them or not!

3. "Receiving the end of your faith, even the salvation of your souls." (1 Peter 1:9.) The word end in this verse means outcome or result. The faith of Christians must be living. If it is not accompanied with works of obedience to God it is as dead as a corpse. (James 2.)

The salvation that will be the end result or outcome of Christian faith was spoken of and written about by Old Testament prophets, but they did not understand what they said about it. So, in the next verse, Peter wrote, "Of which salvation the prophets have inquired and searched diligently, who prophesied of the grace that should come unto you: searching what, or what manner of time the Spirit of Christ which was in them did signify, when it testified beforehand the sufferings of Christ, and the glory that should follow. Unto whom it was revealed, that not unto themselves, but unto us they did minister the things, which are now reported unto you by them which have preached the gospel unto you with the Holy Ghost sent down from heaven; which things the angels desire to look into." (1 Peter 1:10-12.)

Peter obviously meant in these verses that the Old Testament prophets went to school to their own writings about the Messianic age and the blessings of the gospel. They studied their prophecies about Christ and salvation in him, diligently. They wanted to know what they meant, and could not. This proves God did not give them thoughts to express in their own words. He gave them the very words to speak and write, and they spoke and wrote them whether they understood them or not!

4. Speaking as the Spirit gave him utterance (Acts 2:4), the apostle Peter said something on Pentecost he did not believe, so it is doubtful that he understood it. After telling the believing and convicted Jews to repent and be baptized in order to have forgiveness of their sins (Acts 2:38), he said, "For the promise is unto you, and to your children, and to all that are afar off, even as many as the Lord our God shall call." (Acts 2:39.)

"Them that are afar off" of Peter's God given statement refers to the Gentiles. But at that time Peter did not understand or believe that Gentiles should hear the gospel. Ten years later he still did not believe this, for God told him to go to preach to Cornelius and his household who were Gentiles, and Peter did not think he should do so until God convinced him with a miraculous vision that he should. This all means that on Pentecost, Peter truly was guided by the Spirit of God, otherwise he would not have said what he said!

Words Taught By The Holy Spirit
Writing concerning what he taught, the apostle Paul wrote, "Which things also we speak, not in words which man's wisdom teacheth, but which the Holy Ghost teacheth; comparing spiritual things with spiritual." (1 Corinthians 2:13.)
In the foregoing Paul stated by the Holy Spirit why none can write a book as good as, or better than the Bible. The Bible writers wrote words which the Holy Spirit gave them.

Were The Writers or Just the Word Inspired?
Some have said that it is incorrect to refer to the writers of the Bible as "inspired writers." They say those who wrote the Bible were not inspired, but the words which God gave through the writers of the Bible were inspired words, but it is manifestly evident that it can also be truthfully said that the writers were inspired!
The inspired word was in men before the inspired word was in the book called the Bible. We speak freely of a book we call the Bible as "the inspired Bible," because we believe the inspired word of God is in it. But before the inspired word of God was in that book, the inspired word of God was in men. If the inspired word of God being in a book makes that book an inspired book, then the inspired word of God being in men in the sense that God miraculously put it in them, means that they were inspired men!

"Moved By The Holy Ghost"
Referring to Old Testament prophets, Peter wrote that "holy men of God spake as they were moved by the Holy Ghost." (2 Peter 1:21.) I am unable to see any difference between holy men being moved by the Holy Ghost, and holy men being inspired by the Holy Ghost! The word "moved" in Peter's statement is a translation of the Greek word pheromenoi. There are many shades of meaning for this word in the Greek Lexicons, including the concept of being carried along by wind, and being moved by the Spirit of God, and to be under a mov-

ing influence. (See *A Greek-English Lexicon Of The New Testament, and Other Christian Literature* by Arndt, Gingrich, Bauer, and Danker. Also see *The Analytical Greek Lexicon* by Harper Brothers and Samuel Bagster and Sons.)

The reason Bible writers wrote what God wanted them to write was because they were under the moving influence of the Holy Ghost, and the word of God was in them. I believe it is safe, sound, and sensible to say they were inspired, or directed, or moved by the Holy Ghost.

Saying the Bible is inspired of God, but the writers of what is in the Bible were not inspired is like saying mechanic work is skilled labor, but the mechanic who does the work is not skilled.

Some Examples

1. When God instructed Moses to go into Egypt to lead the Israelites out of bondage, he told him, "I will be with thy mouth and with his mouth, and will teach you what ye shall do." (Exodus 4:15.) God meant by this that Moses and Aaron were to say what he directed them to say, or they were to say what God put in them to say.

Writing to Timothy, Paul said what he wrote was also a speaking. "Now the Spirit speaketh expressly that in later times some shall depart from the faith...." (1 Timothy 4:1.) What Paul was writing was what the Spirit was speaking!

We should be thankful that God conveyed his will to us through men. We should thank him for these inspired men!

2. Jesus told his apostles, "But when they deliver you up, take no thought how or what ye shall speak: for it shall be given you in that same hour what ye shall speak. For it is not ye that speak, but the Spirit of your Father which speaketh in you." (Matthew 10:19,20.) This promise is also recorded in Mark 13:11; Luke 12:11,12; and Luke 21:14,15. Those who received these promises had the inspired word in them! All this means that the inspired word was in the men before it was in a book called the New Testament. If the inspired word being in the New Testament means the New Testament is an inspired book, it follows that the inspired word being in men means they were inspired men!

3. The apostle Paul referred to this matter of the inspired word being in men when he wrote, "Now we have received, not the spirit of the world, but the spirit which is of God; that we might know the

things that are freely given to us of God. Which things also we speak, not in the words which man's wisdom teacheth, but which the Holy Ghost teacheth; comparing spiritual things with spiritual." (1 Corinthians 2:12,13.)

Obviously, Paul meant that the words which he received from God were in him and he wrote them.

Questions And Discussion Points

1. What have some said about God's giving thoughts to the Bible writers?

2. Did inspired men understand all they said?

3. Discuss Daniel's statement in the lesson.

4. Let someone relate what Jesus said in Matthew 13 as quoted in the lesson.

5. What is "the end of your faith" in 1 Peter 1:9?

6. What did Peter say Old Testament prophets did relative to their prophecies?

7. Explain what Peter said on Pentecost that he probably did not understand.

8. Is all that is in the Bible easy to understand? Is some of it easy to understand? Is all that is in nature easy to understand? Discuss.

Chapter Twenty

THE HARMONY, CONFIDENCE AND STYLES OF THE BIBLE WRITERS

The Harmony

About forty men were guided by the Holy Spirit to write the Bible. The Bible was written by these during a period of about 1600 years. Some think the Book of Job was the first of the Bible books and that it was written about 1500 to 1600 years before Christ.

Even though the sixty-six books that constitute the one book called the Bible were written by so many writers during so many hundreds of years it is a harmonious volume. This is great evidence that the Bible is of divine origin.

Some have vainly attempted to show that there are contradictions in the Bible. Space does not allow me in this chapter to present some of these so-called contradictions. There are some good books which deal with these and the authors show that what some call contradictions in the Bible are really not contradictions. One of these books is: *Alleged Discrepancies Of The Bible* by John W. Haley. This is an old work, but reprints may still be available from Christian bookstores.

Another valuable book is: *Alleged Bible Contradictions* by my friend of more than 40 years, the late Dr. George W. DeHoff. Perhaps you can get this volume from DeHoff Publications, 749 North West Broad Street, Murfreesboro, TN 37130.

The Confidence

A book of such harmony written over such a long period of time by so many writers is in itself mighty remarkable. Another remarkable matter is the confidence of the writers of the Bible which is so very apparent in their writings on the most intriguing and profound matters. On May 28, 1893, in a speech at the University of Missouri on "The Inspiration Of The Scriptures," the great Christian scholar, J. W. McGarvey said the following on this very point.

"We invite attention next to the air of infallibility which the writers of both Testaments everywhere assume. Though they speak on some themes which have baffled the powers of all thinkers, such as the nature of God, his eternal purposes, his present will, angels, disembodied human spirits, the introduction of sin, the forgiveness and punishment of sin, the future of this earth, and the eternal destiny of us all; on all subjects and on all occasions they speak with a confidence which knows no hesitation, and which admits no possibility of a mistake. Was this the result of stupidity and of overweening self-consciousness? The fact that they are still the teachers of the world on these themes forbids the supposition. Was it the result of a profundity of learning never equaled, or of native powers of insight never approached by the genius of other men? Their positions in society and their want of favorable opportunities forbid this supposition, and our opponents themselves are quick to reject it. What then shall we claim as the cause of it? Grant their miraculous inspiration, and all is plain. There is no other rational hypothesis." (*Sermons*, by J. W. McGarvey, page 12.)

The Styles

Some have objected to the doctrine of the inspiration of the Bible on the grounds that since the writers manifested their individual styles of writing they could not have been divinely guided in the process we call inspiration.

In Chapter Seventeen in this book under the heading, "We Cannot Comprehend The Process Of Inspiration," it was conceded that there are matters about the inspiration of the Bible which we cannot rationalize and explain. One of these maters is how God could direct men to write what he wanted them to write and use the different styles of writing of the writers in doing so.

There is no difficulty in believing that the Almighty and Infinite God used the individual style of each writer in having his book written.

Paul called Luke the beloved physician in Colossians 4:14. Luke wrote *The Gospel According To Luke* and *The Book Of Acts*. Scholars have long been aware of the medical terminology in these two treatises. *The Medical Language Of St. Luke* is a book containing about 300 pages by William Kirk Hobart of Trinity College in Dublin, Ireland. It is a very scholarly book and contains many interesting details about Luke's usage of medical terminology.

"For it is easier for a camel to go through a needle's eye, than for a rich man to enter into the kingdom of God." (Luke 18:25.)

"Needle's eye" of this passage is from **trematos belones**. **Eye of a needle** is a translation in the order of the words of Luke's Greek text. **Eye** is from **trematos** of which Hobart says "the great medical word for a perforation of any kind." **Belone** is the Greek word for a surgical needle.

In the foregoing, "the beloved physician," Luke used the Greek word **belone** for needle. Matthew and Mark used the Greek word **hraphidos** in their accounts of this same statement. **Hraphidos** is the Greek word for a household needle.

There was no problem involved in the Holy Spirit's directing the writers in their use of different words to refer to a needle.

A Common Style

While it is true that each writer of the Bible had his individual style and vocabulary which the Holy Spirit used, it is also true that there are traits and characteristics of the writings in the Bible which suggest that the writers had a common style which was brought about by the influence of the Holy Spirit upon them. In the following quotation from the same sermon already cited, McGarvey makes a good point on this matter.

"Again and again, almost from time immemorial, it has been argued that if the Spirit of God had guided the sacred penmen after the manner affirmed by Paul, all the books would have been written in one style instead of being marked as they are by all the varieties of style and diction which naturally distinguished their respective writers. To this it has been as often answered, that the infinite Spirit of God could as easily guide a number of writers along the course of their own respective styles and within the limits of their own previously acquired knowledge of words, as in any other way. This seems to be a satisfactory answer. But still it must be conceded that if the Spirit of God exercised any direction over the selection by these men of their words, their modes of expression, or the matter of their narrations, it is but natural to suppose that we may find traces of the fact in characteristics which the writings would not otherwise possess – characteristics by which they may be distinguished as inspired writings. I believe that such characteristics can be pointed out, and that, when properly considered, they furnish conclusive proof of the inspiration in question."

They Did Not Conceal Their Own Faults and Sins

When the Bible is closely examined it becomes much harder to believe the writers were not divinely directed in what they wrote than it is to believe they were guided by the Holy Spirit.

One of the characteristics of the writings in the Bible that lends support to the view they were divinely guided in what they wrote is the fact that there is no evidence in their writings that they ever attempted to cover up their own faults and sins and the faults and sins of each other. These are related in the sacred volume with the same fullness of detail and clarity as are the most dastardly deeds of their enemies.

1. Because the people of a Samaritan village did not receive Jesus, two of his apostles, James and John wanted to call down fire from heaven to destroy them. Jesus told them, "Ye know not what manner of spirit ye are of. For the Son of man is not come to destroy men's lives, but to save them." (Luke 9:52-56.)

2. The apostles of Jesus were in a long continuing dispute over who would be greatest in the kingdom of God. Jesus asked them, "What was it that ye disputed among yourselves by the way? But they held their peace: for by the way they had disputed among themselves, who should be the greatest." (Mark 9:33,34.)

"And there was also a strife among them, which of them should be accounted the greatest." (Luke 22:24.)

Ten of the apostles got mad at the other two apostles, James and John, because they requested of Jesus the most prominent positions in the kingdom that Jesus told them was coming. Matthew told that he and the nine other apostles were indignant about this arrogance of James and John. (Matthew 20:20-24.)

At the time the apostles were disputing among themselves and engaged in strife and were indignant, they thought the kingdom of which Jesus often spoke was to be an earthly kingdom. Their misunderstanding and ignorance of this important matter is clearly recorded by some of them in the New Testament.

3. As prominent as he was at the time of their writings, the sacred historians did not shrink back from writing plainly about Peter's cowardice and cursing, and denial of the Lord Jesus. (Matthew 26:69-75; Mark 14:66-72; Luke 22:54-62; John 18:15-27.)

When Peter was one of the main leaders in the church, Paul wrote plainly about something he, Barnabas, and others did that was wrong, and said they were to be blamed and that they walked not uprightly according to the truth. (Galatians 2:9-14.)

Luke wrote about Peter's deep-rooted racial prejudice and ignorance of how the gospel was for all people, and how God helped him to overcome these. (Acts 10.) This was about ten years after Peter preached on Pentecost. (Acts 2.)

4. There are many other cases in the New Testament of attitudes, actions, faults, prejudices, and sins of prominent disciples of Jesus.

One of these is the case of Judas Iscariot, one of the twelve apostles, who betrayed his Lord and sold him out for thirty pieces of silver.

Another case is how all the disciples of Jesus fled away when their Master was arrested not long before he was crucified. (Matthew 26:56.)

The disciples of Jesus lost their hope after Jesus was crucified and buried, and they went fishing. (John 21.)

Some women reported to the apostles of Jesus Christ what they heard the angels say about how Christ had been raised from the dead, and their words seemed to the apostles as idle tales, or foolish words. The apostles did not believe them! (Luke 24:1-11.)

"Now when He rose early on the first day of the week, He appeared first to Mary Magdalene, out of whom He had cast seven demons. She went and told those who had been with Him, as they mourned and wept. And when they heard that He was alive and had been seen by her, they did not believe. After that, He appeared in another form to two of them as they walked and went into the country. And they went and told it to the rest, but they did not believe them either. Afterward He appeared to the eleven as they sat at the table; and He rebuked their unbelief and hardness of heart, because they did not believe those who had seen Him after He had risen. And He said to them, 'Go into all the world and preach the gospel to every creature. He who believes and is baptized will be saved; but he who does not believe will be condemned.'" (Mark 16:9-16.)

The foregoing is an astonishing report that shows that the inspired writer, Mark, did not shrink back from telling that the eleven apostles were rebuked by Jesus for their unbelief and hardness of heart right before He gave them what we call the Great Commission!

If Mark had not been inspired by the Holy Spirit, it is very unlikely he would have told of the unbelief and hardness of heart of the eleven apostles!

Conclusion
The foregoing are only a few of the things the New Testament writers wrote either about themselves or fellow writers and disciples.

The Old Testament also abounds in bad things concerning some of the writers and other prominent leaders among God's people.

It seems very strange indeed that the Bible writers included in their writings such matters if they were imposters and not inspired of God. Had they been uninspired, doubtless they would not have included such matters. It is very unlikely that they would have included such in their writings had they had been writing a story to deceive and mislead and build up a case and a following for themselves!

Questions And Discussion Points

1. During about how many years was the Bible written?

2. What two books on so-called Bible contradictions are mentioned in the lesson? Do you have these?

3. Discuss the statement by J. W. McGarvey.

4. What do some say about the different styles of Bible writers?

5. About what did the apostles fuss? How many of them got mad?

6. Discuss Peter's cowardice and cursing.

7. Name some other cases of faults and sins on the part of servants of Jesus.

8. Are there any cases of such in the Old Testament?

Chapter Twenty-one

THEIR LACK OF EMOTIONALISM AND THEIR AMAZING BREVITY

The writers of the Bible did not write subjectively. They did not allow their writings to be vents for their emotions. There are a few exceptions to this. The Old Testament book of The Lamentations of Jeremiah could be classed as an exception, as well as some of the statements by Jeremiah and others in the Old Testament who expressed vigorously and lamentably their feelings about sin and its consequences. But, there was great purpose in such. God guided them to focus attention on the horrendous nature of sin and disobedience.

A sample of such is in Jeremiah 9:1,2 where the weeping prophet wrote, "Oh that my head were waters, and mine eyes a fountain of tears, that I might weep night and day for the slain of the daughter of my people. Oh that I had in the wilderness a lodging place of wayfaring men; that I might leave my people, and go from them! For they be adulterers, an assembly of treacherous men."

The rebellion and sins of God's people caused Jeremiah to want to get away from them and go into the motel business!

Some Mourned And Wept

Some of the New Testament writers were included in the number of those who mourned and wept over Jesus and what happened to him (Mark 16:10) but they left no sign in their writings that they were mourning and weeping when they wrote about the awful ordeal their Master had endured! To put it poetically we could say there evidently were no tearstains on the pages of what they wrote. This is not to say the holy historians were not emotional, or that they had no feelings about the monumental matters about which they wrote, but it is obvious they did not inject such feelings into what they wrote. This was because the Holy Spirit guided them to write just what God Almighty wanted them to write.

No Great Wonder Expressed

Bible writers did not express their excitement or great wonder in their writings even though they wrote about the most monumental and stupendous events.

1. The report in the Bible about the beheading of John the Baptist was made with the same calmness with which was reported his "crying in the wilderness." (Matthew 14.)

2. The scourging and agony of the crucifixion is reported by New Testament writers just like they told of his mother and his brethren asking to see him when he was teaching, and many other such events and incidents. There are no pathetic exaggerations in the sacred accounts about the sufferings of the Savior. The New Testament writers did not get carried away by sentiment or sympathy when they wrote about the awful ordeal their Master endured. They did not magnify the pathos of what happened on Golgotha by writing strong and long statements about how they felt about it all. Instead they just stated the facts about what happened in a manner that made it apparent they were not recording their own feelings and views, but what God wanted them to write!

3. Even though the enemies of Jesus and his followers were bold and cruel, the writers of the New Testament wrote no harsh and vehement editorials against them. They did not write such against Governor Pilate, nor the chief priests, nor the mob that insisted on Jesus being crucified, nor the Roman soldiers who executed Jesus, nor even the Emperor of Rome for allowing such a ghastly event to take place.

4. The writers of the New Testament did not even express their admiration for the preaching of Jesus. One of them did record what some of the enemies of Jesus said about the Lord's speaking. They said, "Never a man spake like this man." (John 7:46.)

5. The New Testament writers did not include in that sacred volume exaggerations and rigorous statements or long drawn out treatises in which they expressed their feelings about the character of Jesus. Instead they stated just the facts about his flawless character and his sinlessly perfect life!

Peter said of the Savior "he went about doing good" (Acts 10:38) and that "he did no sin, neither was guile found in his mouth: who when he was reviled, reviled not again; when he suffered he threatened not: but committed himself to him that judgeth righteously; who his own self bare our sins in his own body on the tree, that we being dead to sins, should live unto righteousness: by whose stripes ye were healed." (1 Peter 2:22-24.)

6. The writers of the New Testament did not exclaim their feelings or excitement about the miracles their Master performed or

about the miracles their Master caused them to perform. They just calmly stated that these miracles occurred!

7. The New Testament writers wrote unemotionally about the mangled dead body of their Master being placed in a cold tomb. They wrote calmly of his resurrection on the third day. They did not write long exultations of his being raised from the dead. They stated that fact plainly and simply! This is also true of his ascension. They wrote not about their feelings about the death, burial, and resurrection of their Master, and of his appearances to many after his resurrection, and his ascension to heaven. Instead they just calmly stated that these monumental and colossal events took place!

The very unusual style of the Bible writers truly lends tremendous support to the doctrine of the inspiration of this blessed volume.

The Amazing Brevity!

Another mark of the common style of the Bible writers is the amazing brevity of what they wrote about the most monumental matters. They may not have realized it as they began to write what they wrote in the Bible, but the eternal well being of all people who would ever live depended on what they would write!

There were many wondrous details which the sacred scribes could put into the record! What would they write? What would they leave out? Fortunately, they did not have to make such a decision. The Holy Spirit would guide them wisely in all this.

Great Events In The Old Testament

In what are about 50 pages of an average sized book, Moses wrote in Genesis, history covering about 2500 years.

1. Moses wrote about the creation of the heavens, the earth, and all that is in them, in two short chapters, plus a few brief statements in other chapters.

An imaginative and creative writer could have written a book bigger than the Bible on the creative work of God about just one of the six days of creation. Moses wrote about all six days of God's creation of all things on what we could call three or four pages. This fact supports the idea that he must have been guided by the Creator to write just what the Creator wanted in the record!

2. I have three rather large books about the great flood about which Moses wrote in Genesis. I have no way of estimating how

much has been written by uninspired men about the flood of Genesis. But Moses wrote three or four pages about it, and other Bible writers made a few brief statements about this universal deluge. This astounding brevity in the Bible about such a great event lends great support to the doctrine that God Almighty guided the men who wrote the Bible to write what they wrote in that amazing book!

3. The story of the crossing of the Red Sea is another example of the brevity of the writings in the Bible about great events. A good writer could have written a book bigger than the Bible about this colossal event, but Moses reported it on about one page! Uninspired men spent much time and perhaps millions of dollars depicting an imitation of the crossing of the Red Sea in a great movie entitled **The Ten Commandments**, but God recorded the event on a small piece of writing material in a desolate land through a man called Moses!

Great Events In The New Testament

1. The birth of the Son of God! What a story! No person nor group of persons could even estimate how much uninspired people have written about the birth of Jesus. But the Holy Spirit guided writers put in the New Testament only a few words about this monumental event. More has been written in songs about it than is written in the Bible about it!

Matthew wrote a few words about the virgin Mary giving birth to Jesus. Luke made a relatively short statement about it. Mark did not even mention it. John referred to it by merely saying, "And the Word was made flesh and dwelt among us, (and we beheld his glory, the glory as of the only begotten of the Father,) full of grace and truth." (John 1:14.)

It is obvious that those who wrote the New Testament were not ordinary uninspired scribes, but they wrote as the Spirit of God directed them!

2. God spoke from heaven while the Holy Spirit descended from heaven in the form of a dove, and Jesus was coming out of the water of Jordan. What a scene! What an event! A good writer could have written a large book on this event. But all that the divinely guided scribes wrote about it could be written on a postal card!

3. Very brief accounts are given in the New Testament of the scene of the transfiguration of Jesus on the holy mount when Moses and Elijah were summoned by the Almighty from the spirit world and

appeared with Jesus. This would be a good subject for a good sized book, but holy writers wrote just a few words about it!

4. The New Testament writers wrote relatively little about the life of Jesus. They wrote mostly about the last three years he was on the earth. Mark and John did not even mention the first 30 years of our Lord's life. Matthew and Luke wrote very little of the early years of Jesus. No New Testament writer tells of anything in the life of Jesus from the time he was about twelve years old until he was thirty.

5. All that is written in the New Testament about the crucifixion of Jesus when he gave his life a ransom for all, is contained on a few small pages in the sacred volume. The same can be said of the resurrection of Jesus. These events are the subjects of many large gooks. Over forty years ago I wrote a small book on the resurrection of Jesus entitled *What Happened To The Body?* I am in the process of enlarging it and publishing it in much larger form.

6. The ascension from earth to heaven of our Lord Jesus Christ is told in very few words in the New Testament.

7. Other significant events, and even tragic matters are reported very briefly in the New Testament.

The death of Stephen, the first martyr in the church is recorded in just a few words. (Acts 7.)

The death of the apostle James is reported in Acts 12:2. What were his last words? How did he act? A great Christian leader was murdered! He was the brother of John the apostle of love! A large volume could have been written about this tragic event, yet Luke reported it in seven Greek words in Acts 12:2!

The Bible is the word of God!

(Some of the ideas of this chapter are from the lesson by J. W. McGarvey cited in Chapter Twenty.)

Questions And Discussion Points

What is meant by the title of the lesson?

What are some exceptions?

Discuss what is said about Mark 16:10.

4. What emotionally charged event was calmly recorded in Matthew 14?

5. Discuss how the crucifixion of Jesus is reported in the New Testament.

Discuss the brevity of the Genesis account of creation.

Discuss the brevity of Moses' account of the crossing of the Red Sea.

Compare the Genesis account of the great flood with how much uninspired men have written about it.

Chapter Twenty-two

PROFOUND OBSERVATIONS ON THE NEW TESTAMENT

It has been my observation for more than half a century that many good people use better judgment and reason about most any matter than they use in their attitude toward the Bible and their endeavors to go to heaven. Many do not take the Bible seriously enough, and are very subjective in their religion.

Saving faith comes by hearing or learning the Word of God (Romans 10:14-17) and it is very reasonable. Believing what one has to believe if he does not believe the Bible is unreasonable belief! This is true of both the Old Testament and the New Testament.

The following are sound and profound observations which focus on the New Testament. These should challenge all to take that Book very seriously!

1. It is overflowing with sublime and correct views of theology, **none of which has been disproven!**

2. It presents the true character of people without flattery, distortion, or exaggeration!

3. It has an astonishing power of penetrating the human heart, and conscience!

4. It gives us abundant information on the very points **with which it is most important we be acquainted!**

5. It opens to us the future world and **clearly shows how we may obtain its happiness and eternal glory!**

6. **This blessed book – the New Testament** – exhibits a perfect system of moral responsibility and duty **which works** in the lives of all who follow it!

7. This book **forbids nothing in morality except what will harm us!**

8. It requires nothing that is not reasonable and virtuous!

9. It addresses all people in every relation of life on the matters that are most important to a good life in this world and in the world to come!

10. The New Testament presents the character of **its principal person – Jesus Christ of Nazareth**, the founder of Christianity, with such perfection of moral excellency by telling us his words, his

deeds, and his sufferings, that nothing can be taken from it, or added to it without detracting from its worth!

11. A sane person cannot say this book – **The New Testament** – is the production of impostors!

12. If the New Testament was written by men who not only were not inspired of God, but were impostors and deceivers and wrote what they knew was not so:

(1) Why did they not make some serious blunders- at least one – in their theology and/or their morality?

(2) How did they maintain such beautiful harmony and consistency in all the book called the New Testament?

(3) How did they present such a perfect character as that of Jesus? The great American Historian and prolific writer, Will Durant, who was not a Bible apologist, confronted this question and responded as follows. "That a few simple men should in one generation have invented so appealing a personality, so lofty an ethic and so inspiring a vision of human brotherhood, would be a miracle far more incredible than any recorded in the Gospels." (*The Story of Civilization*, Volume 3, Christ and Caesar, page 557.) Obviously, Durant meant that the writers of the New Testament did not invent Jesus!

(4) If The New Testament writers were vile impostors how did they present Jesus always acting and speaking in all circumstances – difficult as well as those not difficult – **without ever ascribing to him any error or weakness in word or deed?**

(5) If The New Testament writers were **impostors and deceivers** why did they denounce all manner of falsehood and deceit as is done in the New Testament?

(6) Why did they insist so much on holiness, even in the thoughts and purposes of the heart?

(7) If The New Testament writers were impostors how did they so perfectly adapt their forgery to the constitution of the human mind and circumstances of people?

(8) What person even, in this modern age of learning and technology, could **compose even the discourses**, said by The New Testament writers to have been presented by Jesus of Nazareth?

In the foregoing comments I have incorporated some thoughts from Dr. Archibald Alexander from his book on Christian Evidences. He founded Princeton Theological Seminary in 1812 and was with that school until he died in 1852. While he was there that school was very conservative, and it was for quite some time after he died.

Comments By Channing About Chrsit Not Being Invented

Dr. William E. Channing eloquently and very logically defended the New Testament and its portrayal of Christ in the following.

"Perhaps it may be said this character never existed. Then the invention of it is to be explained, and the reception which this fiction met with; and these perhaps are as difficult of explanation on natural principles as its real existence.

"Christ's history bears all the marks of reality; a more frank, simple, unlabored, unostentatious narrative was never penned. Besides, his character, if invented, must have been an invention of singular difficulty, because no models existed on which to frame it. He stands alone in the records of time. The conception of a being, proposing such new and exalted ends, and governed by higher principles than the progress of society had developed, implies singular intellectual power.

"That several individuals should join in equally vivid conceptions of this character, and should not merely describe in general terms the fictitious being to whom it was attributed, but should introduce him into real life, should place him in a great variety of circumstances, in connection with various ranks of men, with friends and foes, and should in all preserve his identity, show the same great and singular mind always acting in harmony with itself; this is a supposition hardly credible, and, when the circumstances of the writers of the New Testament are considered, seems to be as inexplicable on human principles as what I before suggested, the composition of Newton's 'Principia' by a savage.

"The character of Christ, though delineated in an age of great moral darkness, has stood the scrutiny of ages; and, in proportion as men's moral sentiments have been refined, its beauty has been more seen and felt. To suppose it was invented is to suppose that its authors, outstripping their age, had attained to a singular delicacy and elevation of moral perception and feeling. But these attainments are not very reconcilable with the character of its authors, supposing it to be a fiction; that is, with the character of habitual liars and impious deceivers.

"But we are not only unable to discover powers adequate to this invention. There must have been motives for it; for men do not make great efforts without strong motives; and, in the whole compass of human incitements, we challenge the infidel to suggest any which could have prompted to the work now to be explained.

"Once more, it must be recollected that this invention, if it were one, was received as real at a period so near to the time ascribed to Christ's appearance that the means of detecting it were infinite. That men should send out such a forgery, and that it should prevail and triumph, are circumstances not easily reconcilable with the principles of our nature.

"The character of Christ, then, was real. Its reality is the only explanation of the mighty revolution produced by his religion. And how can you account for it, but by that cause to which he always referred it, - a mission from the Father?" (*The Works Of William E. Channing*, D.D., page 229; Boston, American Unitarian Association, 1877.)

Conclusion

The cardinal principles and profound truths about the New Testament in this chapter should be very convincing to all skeptics that the standard of values and morality taught in that book is far superior to all heathen codes of conduct! How can we account for that superiority?

1. We cannot account for it by affirming that the writers of the New Testament had superior mental powers. In this regard it is doubtful that they excelled the ancient Greeks and Romans whose moral systems brought upon them social devastation and many accompanying woes.

2. It was not because the New Testament writers had superior education in matters pertaining to secular and social order. The ancient heathen philosophers spared little in acquiring such knowledge, and they did not produce a book any where near being comparable to the New Testament!

It is altogether logical and reasonable to conclude that the morality of the Bible, and the Bible itself is from God!

God's Word

I paused last eve beside the blacksmith's door,
And heard the anvil ring, the vesper's chime,
And looking in I saw upon the floor
Old hammers, worn with beating years of time.

"How many anvils have you had?" said I,
"To wear and batter all these hammers so?"
"Just one," he answered. Then with twinkling eye:
"The anvil wears the hammers out, you know."

And so, I thought, the anvil of God's Word
For ages skeptics' blows have beat upon,
But though the noise of falling blows was heard
The anvil is unchanged; the hammers gone.

John Clifford
1836-1923

Questions And Discussion Notes

What does the chapter say is "unreasonable belief?"

Discuss each of the 12 "profound observations" which focus on the New Testament that are in the chapter.

What did Will Durant say about the writers of the New Testament?

What is the main thrust of the comments by Dr. William Channing?

What are at least five implications if the New Testament writers were impostors?

Is there any evidence that the New Testament writers had superior mental powers?

Did the New Testament writers have more education than others? Discuss.

Let someone read John Clifford's poem and comment on it.

Chapter Twenty-three

IS MARK 16:9-20 PART OF
THE SACRED CANON?

About 6000 ancient Greek manuscripts of the New Testament, many of which are not complete, have been found. Two of these are Codex Vaticanus and Codex Sinaiticus which scholars say were made in the fourth century. Mark 16:9-20 is not in these, but there are many evidences these verses should be in these manuscripts. The Vaticanus has a blank space where these verses should be and is big enough to contain them. Some scholars think the scribe forgot to put them in the space.

Verses 14-16 of Mark 16 say, "Afterward He appeared to the eleven as they sat at the table; and he rebuked their unbelief and hardness of heart, because they did not believe those who had seen him after He had risen. And he said unto them, 'Go into all the world and preach the gospel to every creature. He who believes and is baptized will be saved; but he who does not believe will be condemned.'"

I have heard men whom I debated and men whom others debated, contend in those debates that Mark 16:9-20 is not a part of the Bible because the two ancient manuscripts mentioned above do not contain these verses. They did this to try to prove that baptism is not essential to salvation. They evidently did not realize their attempt was an admission that Mark 16:15,16 teaches that baptism is essential to salvation, otherwise why did they bother with trying to prove these verses are not part of the Bible?

If Mark 16:14-16 actually were not part of the Bible, we would still know that baptism is essential to salvation because there are many other New Testament scriptures which clearly teach that baptism is essential to salvation through the blood of Jesus Christ! Some of these passages are: John 3:5; Acts 2:38; 22:16; Romans 6:3-5; Galatians 3:26,27; and 1 Peter 3:20-22.

Those who deny that baptism is essential to salvation should take no comfort in the fact that the words of Jesus that "He that believeth and is baptized shall be saved," are not in the 4th century Vaticanus and Sinaiticus manuscripts, because those words are in most ancient Greek manuscripts of the New Testament, and they are in all the ancient translations of the Greek New Testament into several other languages.

The oldest known Greek manuscripts of the New Testament are not as old as some translations made from the Greek New Testament. Some of these translations are: the Peshito (common language) Syriac; the Old Latin; and the Egyptian Coptic. The Coptic translations were made into six dialects. **These were made beginning in the Second Century and therefore about 200 years older than the Sinaiticus and Vaticanus manuscripts, and they all have Mark 16:9-20 in them!**

Testimony From J. W. McGarvey

The eminent Christian scholar, J. W. McGarvey who died in 1911, commented on Mark 16:9-20 in his *Commentary On Matthew And Mark*. He wrote: "It was also cited by Irenaeus and Tatian of the second century, all of whom lived before the earliest existing manuscript was written and from one hundred years earlier than Jerome. The words of Irenaeus show that it was not only a part of the book of Mark in his day, but that Mark was regarded as its author."

John W. Burgon And His Book On Mark 16:9-20

John W. Burgon was born in 1813 and died in 1888. Most of his adult life was spent at Oxford University in England as Fellow of Oriel College, as "Vicar of St. Mary's Church" (the Oxford University Church of England), and "Gresham Professor of Divinity." The last twelve years of his life he was "Dean of Chichester." Even though I do not agree with some of the religious views he and others at Oxford held, I must say, Dean Burgon was not a dummy! It would have been a treat to hear how he would have responded to the preachers whom I and others debated who contended that Mark 16:15,16 is not a part of the Bible!

Burgon wrote a very scholarly, well documented book entitled *The Last Twelve Verses Of Mark* in which he presents a very adequate array of evidence that Mark 16:9-20 is indeed a part of the word of God!

Dr. Edward F. Hills, a graduate of both Yale and Harvard wrote the Introduction to Burgon's book. Among many other commendations of Burgon in that Introduction, he wrote, "The thing about Burgon, however, which lifts him out of his nineteenth century English setting and endears him to the hearts of earnest Christians of other lands and other ages is his steadfast defence of the Scripture as the infallible Word of God. He strove with all his power to arrest the modernistic currents which during his lifetime had begun to flow within the Church of England, continuing his efforts with unabated zeal up to the very day of his death. With this purpose in mind he labored mightily in the field of New Testament textual criticism."

Burgon On The Testimony Of Early "Church Fathers" On Mark 16:9-20

"Early Church Fathers" refers to high caliber leaders, spokesmen, writers, and scholars in the church of the first three or four centuries.

On page 79 of his book, John Burgon wrote, "It shall be my endeavour in the ensuing pages to shew, on the contrary, that manuscript evidence is so overwhelmingly in their favour that no room is left for doubt or suspicion: that **there is not so much as one of the Fathers, early or late, who gives it as his opinion that these verses are spurious; and, that the argument derived from internal considerations proves on inquiry to be baseless and unsubstantial as a dream.**"

Burgon names and comments on quite a number of these "Fathers." Justin Martyr is one of them, who in his first *Apology*, written in 150 A.D., quoted part of Mark 16:20, and did not indicate that there was any question about the authenticity of the last twelve verses of Mark 16.

Burgon also names Irenaeus of Lyons another church Father, and says that in his third book *Against Heresies*, written about 180 A.D., he quotes Mark 16:19 and comments on it. This shows that long before the Vaticanus and Sinaiticus manuscripts existed the last twelve verses of Mark 16 were being quoted and used.

Another Church Father was Hippolytus who was one of Irenaeus' contemporaries. Burgon shows that he quoted from the last twelve verses of Mark 16 quite a number of times in several of his writings.

Vincentius, another Church Father of the third century quoted from the last twelve verses of Mark at the Seventh Council of Carthage, according to Dean Burgon.

According to Burgon, Ambrose of Milan, John Chrysostom, Jerome who translated the Bible into Latin, Augustine, and numbers of others of the fourth and fifth centuries quoted freely from Mark 16:9-20.

In the Introduction to the Book of Mark in *The Pulpit Commentary*, (Vol. 16) the writer says Justin Martyr of the Second

Century A.D. quotes Mark 16:19,20. Referring to Mark 16:9-20, he says "on the whole, the evidence as to the genuineness and authenticity of this passage seems irresistible."

Heinrich A. W. Meyer, an outstanding scholar said of Mark 16:9-20, "Among English and American writers we may note that the passage is regarded as genuine by Broadus, Burgon, Scrivener, Wordsworth, McClellan, Cook, and Morison." (*Critical And Exegitical Handbook On The Gospels Of Mark And Luke* by Heinrich A. W. Meyer, page 198. First printed in 1883. Reprinted in 1980, by Alpha Publications, Winona Lake, IN.)

The Early New Testament Translations

John Burgon presents an abundance of evidence that the many early translations of the New Testament, already named and discussed in this book in the chapter on the Canon of the New Testament, are strong evidence that Mark 16:9-20 is indeed a part of God's word, because these verses are in those early translations. The reason for this is that these early translations are much older than any of the approximately 6000 ancient Greek manuscripts of the New Testament, including Codex Vaticanus and Codex Sinaiticus!

Yes indeed, you can be assured that Jesus really said, "Go into all the world and preach the gospel to every creature. He that believeth and is baptized shall be saved," because this scripture is part of God's eternal word. No amount of arguing and trying to get around what it says will change what it says, or destroy what it says.

If someone told you a story and then told you if you would believe the story and be baptized he would give you a new automobile, would you expect to receive the car without being baptized? I think not!

Attempts To Get Around Baptism

Satan surely knows Mark 16:9-20 is a part of God's word. He must surely be pleased by the attempts so many false teachers have made to try to prove this text is not part of the Word of God. Their purpose is to try to get around the idea that baptism is essential to being saved, because in verses 15, 16 Jesus said to his apostles, "Go ye into all the world, and preach the gospel to every creature. He that believeth and is baptized shall be saved; but he that believeth not shall be damned."

"He" of this text is generic; it includes males and females. He is a translation of the Greek article "ho" which means "the one," or "the person." Obviously it means the person who is lost.

Some have contended that Jesus did not say, "he that is not baptized shall be damned." We should all be glad he did not say that, for if he had that would have disqualified him from being "the Master Teacher."

Suppose Jesus had said, "He that hears the gospel and believes it shall be saved, but he who does not hear the gospel and does not believe it shall be damned." It is obvious that if one does not hear (or learn) the gospel he cannot believe it.

It only takes not believing the gospel to be lost, but it takes more than believing the gospel to be saved!

If one said, "He that eats food and digests it shall live, but he that does not eat food and does not digest it will die," he would sound stupid. It is obvious that one will not digest what he does not eat! It takes more than eating food to live, but just not eating food will cause one to die!

It would be ridiculous for one to say, "He that enrolls in college and makes passing grades will graduate, but he that does not enroll in college and does not make passing grades will not graduate."

"And Jesus said unto them, Ye are from beneath; I am from above: ye are of this world; I am not of this world. I said therefore unto you, that ye shall die in your sins: for if you believe not that I am *he*, ye shall die in your sins." (John 8:23,24.)

Observe that "he" of verse 24 is italicized which means there is no word for it in the Greek text. This means that Jesus meant "I am from above, and if you do not believe I am, you shall die in your sins!"

To be lost all one has to do is not believe that Jesus is from above! Just refuse to believe that Jesus came down from heaven (John 6:38), or refuse to believe he came forth from the Father (John 16:28) and you will be lost!

"He that believeth and is baptized shall be saved" (Mark 16:16); "Repent and be baptized in the name of Jesus Christ for the remission of sins" (Acts 2:38); "Arise and be baptized and wash away thy sins (Acts 22:16); and "Baptism doth also now save us (1 Peter 3:21), all refer to the same thing. "Shall be saved"; "for remission of sins"; "wash away thy sins"; and "saves us" of these texts all mean the same thing. There are many other New Testament passages that teach that those who are not Christians must be baptized to be saved and thus become Christians. The thousands of preachers and others who say baptism is not essential do not change what God's word says! So be it!

Questions And Discussion Points

About how many ancient Greek manuscripts of the New Testament have been discovered?

What two of them do not contain Mark 16:9-20?

Are there any translations of the New Testament older than the oldest Greek manuscripts of the New Testament?

What did J. W. McGarvey say about Irenaeus?

Who was John Burgon? Did he think Mark 16:9-20 was a part of God's word?

Who was Edward F. Hills?

Did any "church Fathers" recognize Mark 16:9-20 as part of the Sacred Canon?

What is said about an automobile in the lesson?

Chapter Twenty-four

"RIGHTLY DIVIDING," "OR HANDLING ARIGHT" THE WORD OF TRUTH

The following are seven translations of 2 Timothy 2:15.

"Study to shew thyself approved unto God, a workman that needeth not to be ashamed, rightly dividing the word of truth." – King James Version

"Be diligent to present yourself approved to God, a worker who does not need to be ashamed, rightly dividing the word of truth." – New King James Version

"Give diligence to present thyself approved unto God, a workman that needeth not to be ashamed, handling aright the word of truth." – American Standard Version

"Be diligent to present yourself approved to God as a workman who does not need to be ashamed, handling accurately the word of truth." – New American Version

"Do your best to present yourself to God an approved workman who has nothing to be ashamed of, who properly presents the message of the truth." – Dr. Charles B. Williams Version

"Do your best to present yourself to God as one approved, a workman who does not need to be ashamed and who correctly handles the word of truth." – New International Version

"Be eager thyself approved to present to God, a workman unashamed, cutting straight the word of the truth." – This is a translation according to the literal order or arrangement of the words of the Greek text, by Dr. Alfred Marshall.

Please observe that "**worker**" is in the NKJV, and "**workman**" is in the other six. Both are good translations of the Greek word "**ergaten**" from which they are translated in the text. Studying, or giving diligence and properly handling, or using, or teaching the word of truth does, indeed, require work! I often told the hundreds of preacher students I have taught there are no ten easy lessons to becoming a good preacher, or to becoming a workman approved of God!

The Greek word "**spoudasin**" is translated "study," and several other ways in the seven versions shown above. "**Spoudasin**" is a form of "**speudo**" which has many connotations, including, urgency, eagerness, haste, earnestness, and diligence. When Jesus told

Zacchaeus to "**make haste**" and come down out of the sycamore tree, and Zacchaeus "made haste and came down," a form of "**speudo**" is translated "**haste**." (Luke 19:5,6.) The Lord told Paul to "make haste and get thee quickly out of Jerusalem." (Acts 22:18.) "**Make haste**" in that command is translated from a form of "**speudo**."

The lexicons I checked do not include "**study**" as a meaning of "**spoudasin**." However one could not do what the word means without studying. However, "**spoudasin**" emphasizes or focuses on the haste, the urgency, and the diligence involved in what the Holy Spirit enjoins in Paul's charge! Therefore, for a gospel preacher, or any Christian, it is always an urgent matter to study God's word for many reasons. One of these was stated by the holy writer in Psalm 119:11, when he addressed the Almighty and said "Your word I have hidden in my heart, that I might not sin against you." About 1968 I heard my dear friend Charles R. Brewer preach a sermon on this text in which he made three main points which were as follows. 1. The greatest thing, God's word. 2. The greatest place for that greatest thing, my heart. 3. The greatest purpose for the greatest thing to be in the greatest place, that I might not sin against God!

What Is "The Word Of Truth"?

Please notice that "the word of truth" is in all but one of the seven translations of 2 Timothy 2:15. "The message of truth" in Dr. Williams' translation is just as accurate as "the word of truth."

Paul equated "the word of truth" and "the gospel of your salvation." (Ephesians 1:13.) The New Testament gives great emphasis to "the truth" which is the gospel of Jesus Christ. Some of this emphasis is in Paul's two letters to young Timothy. He said God desires all lost people to be saved and to do so they must come to the knowledge of the truth. (1 Timothy 2:4.) In verse 7 he said he spoke the truth, and that he was a teacher of the Gentiles in faith and truth. In 3:15 he told Timothy the church is the pillar and ground of the truth! In 4:3 Paul said the food God gives us is to be received with thanksgiving by those who believe and know the truth. In 6:5 he said men of corrupt minds are destitute of the truth.

Right after he referred to the word of truth in 2 Timothy 2:15, he charged Timothy to shun profane and vain babblings, because such will spread like a cancer. He said Hymenaeus and Philetus were spreading such and that they had strayed concerning the truth. In verse 25 he expressed concern about some because they did not know the truth! In 3:7 Paul said some were ever learning, but had not learned the truth, and in verse 8 he said they resisted the truth! How sad, indeed, that many spend their lives learning, but never learn that which they most of all need to know, the truth! In chapter 4, Paul prophesied there would be a great apostasy of the church because people would turn away from the truth!

What Paul wrote about the truth in his two letters to Timothy is barely "a drop in the bucket" of all that the New Testament teaches regarding the purpose and value of the truth. It is no wonder, therefore, that Paul told Timothy to give diligence to fill his heart with the truth and correctly handle it in his efforts to teach others. Paul told the young preacher to work at being diligent in learning and in handling the truth skillfully. This should cause all preachers and all other Christians to be urgent in learning more of the truth and how to handle it!

What Does "Rightly Divide" or "Handle Aright" Mean?

1. Did Paul mean we should use tact in our efforts of handling the word of truth?

What is tact? Abraham Lincoln said it is the ability to describe others as they see themselves. Another said tact is the ability to make advice agreeable. Someone said it is looking around to be sure no one is related to the person about whom you are going to gossip. Another said tact is the ability to close your mouth before someone else wants to.

I have heard many stories of some who were not tactful. One is about a bachelor minister who conducted a funeral. He rode in a car with the weeping widow to and from the cemetery. Going from the cemetery, he told the widow he needed a wife, and that he wanted her to marry him. She replied, "I'm sorry, but the undertaker has already asked me."

Will Rogers got by with his humor, even if it was not adorned with tact. He addressed a large assembly of bankers in New York City, and began by looking over the august assembly considerably and then said, "This is as good looking a bunch of bankers as ever foreclosed on a widow." The audience roared with laughter.

I heard a preacher friend, Gus Nichols, say a barber got very religious on a weekend. On Monday, the first man who came into his shop wanted a shave. The barber was overflowing with zeal to tell others about salvation. When he got the man's beard lathered, he held his razor over the bearded man's face, and looked into his eyes and asked him, "My friend are you prepared to die?" A good question, indeed, at the proper time, but that was not the proper time!

Gospel preachers and all other Christians should be tactful when they tell others the gospel or the word of truth. Even when we speak tactfully the truth, some may be offended. We should never compromise the truth, but we should not be rude, gruff or surly in presenting it. We should not be unkind. Kindness is not compromise. We should never tell anyone he is an ignoramus in order for him to listen to the truth. We should never be sarcastic while trying to lead someone to Christ.

Paul told the Christians in Colosse, "Walk in wisdom toward those who are outside, redeeming the time. Let your speech always be with grace, seasoned with salt, that you may know how you ought to answer each one." (Colossians 4:5,6.) We should all really work at being as sure as we can be that if people are offended it is the truth that offends them and not the manner of our presenting it, and not the attitude we have in presenting it!

Tact is important in our handling the word of truth, but I am persuaded that is not the main meaning of "handling aright" or "rightly dividing" in 2 Timothy 2:15.

2. Does the passage mean we should be aware of the divisions of the Bible?

There are several ways the Bible is divided. The two primary divisions are the Old Testament and the New Testament. It is very important to know the differences in them. It is also important to know the three ages or dispensations about which the Bible tells us. They are: (1) The Patriarchial Dispensation; (2) The Mosaic Dispensation; and (3) The Christian Dispensation.

The Bible is a spiritual library of 66 divisions known as books. There are 39 such sections in the Old Testament, and 27 in the New Testament.

Some have made divisions in the Old Testament by saying there are books of law; books of history; books of poetry; and books of prophecy in it. This is true only in a general way. For an example the first five books of the Old Testament known as the Pentateuch contain much history even though they are not classified by some as books of history.

The New Testament has also been divided by some as containing books of history, epistles or letters to Christians and churches, and the book of prophecy called Revelation. These divisions of the New Testament must be considered only in a general way. For an example Matthew, Mark, Luke, John, and Acts which are called books of history also contain many great principles and laws of life that are very vital in living the fullest life possible. For an example Matthew's "book of history" of the life of Jesus contains what people call "The Sermon On The Mount." It is in chapters five, six, and seven. What we call "the beatitudes" are in chapter five. These and many other principles and laws of life are in the three chapters. Therefore I would not call these history even though they are in the Book of Matthew which in a general way is a history of the birth, life, death, burial and resurrection of Jesus Christ. I have often called "The Sermon On The Mount," "The Constitution of Christianity," because in it are so many of the basic principles for living the Christian life.

Even though it is important for us to be aware of the various divisions, sections and classifications of the contents of The Book, I do not believe that is the meaning of "handling aright," or "rightly dividing the word of truth."

3. Does the charge mean that when we teach and preach the word of truth we should do so with awareness of the people of various age groups and levels of understanding, and that we should present proper portions each time?

Preachers and teachers of the word of God certainly should be keenly aware that it is very important to teach or handle the word of truth in a manner adapted to the various age and understanding levels of those being taught, including "newborn babes." (1 Peter 2:1-3.) Some are more mature than others. (Hebrews 5:12,13.) Some are not Christians, and these may have different levels of understanding. Some are less aware of "the terror of the Lord" than others, and need to be made aware of the awful consequences of disobedience to God! (2 Corinthians 5:11; 2 Thessalonians 1:3-10.)

Preachers and teachers of the word of truth should work at presenting it in as plain and simple a manner as they can. N. B. Hardeman told us in classes over 50 years ago to do this. He was a master at this. He said, "Boys, put it down where the calves can get it, and the old cows will still be able to get it."

There are times when people need the "comfort of the scriptures" (Romans 15:4) to encourage them. After Paul expounded upon the coming of Christ and the resurrection of the dead loved ones of Christians in the church of the Thessalonians, he told them, "Therefore comfort one another with these words." (1 Thessalonians 4:18.) Often this is done at funerals, but Paul was not preaching a funeral when he wrote 1 Thessalonians! Christians should comfort one another "with these words" of hope regularly!

"Blessed be the God and Father of our Lord Jesus Christ, the Father of mercies and God of all comfort, who comforts us in all our tribulation, that we may be able to comfort those who are in any trouble, with the comfort with which we ourselves are comforted by God. For as the sufferings of Christ abound in us, so our consolation also abounds through Christ. Now if we are afflicted, it is for your consolation and salvation, which is effective for enduring the same sufferings which we also suffer. Or if we are comforted, it is for your consolation and salvation. And our hope for you is steadfast, because we know that as you are partakers of the sufferings, so also you will partake of the consolation." (2 Corinthians 1:3-7.)

No wonder Paul said Christians are saved by hope! (Romans 8:24.) The "one hope" (Ephesians 4:4) is great motivation for those who serve God. Without the hope of the gospel, all the rest of it would mean nothing as far as eternity is concerned.

As important as it is for preachers and teachers of the gospel, those who handle the word of truth, to be aware of the need to recognize the various categories, levels of understanding, and needs of those who hear the word, I do not believe that this is what the Holy Spirit meant in Paul's instruction to Timothy to "handle aright," or "Rightly divide the word of truth." In this chapter I have stated what I do not believe he meant. In the next two chapters I demonstrate what I believe he did mean.

Questions And Discussion Points

1. Read and compare the seven translations of 2 Timothy 2:15.

2. What is "spoudasin"?

3. Discuss the three main points of Psalm 119:11 as Charles Brewer preached on the verse.

4. What did Abraham Lincoln say tact is?

5. What is said in the chapter about Will Rogers?

6. What is meant in the chapter by "The Constitution of Christianity"?

7. What is in the chapter about N.B. Hardeman?

8. Discuss 2 Corinthians 1:3-7.

Chapter Twenty-five

"RIGHTLY DIVIDING," "OR HANDLING ARIGHT" OR "CUTTING STRAIGHT" THE WORD OF TRUTH

The science of interpretation is called "hermeneutics." This word is from Hermes the son of the chief god Zeus and his wife Maia in Greek mythology. Hermes was the messenger of the other gods, and also the god of science, commerce, eloquence, and guide of departing souls into Hades, in the imaginations of idolaters. The Greek and the Roman idolaters had the same imaginary gods but gave them different names.

Luke wrote about Paul and Barnabas being in Lystra where Paul healed a man who had been a cripple all his life. The idolaters there thought Barnabas was the chief god Jupiter, and they thought Paul was Mercurius "because he was the chief speaker." (Acts 14:8-12.) "Mercurius" in the King James Version is the translation of Greek "Hermes." The Romans called this god "Mercurius" and the Greeks called him "Hermes." The New King James Version has "Hermes" in that text instead of "Mercurius." **24**

At the beginning of chapter ~~eleven~~ in this book are several translations of 2 Timothy 2:15. In that chapter are some truths about the Bible that need to be understood, but it is doubtful that Paul's charge in 2 Timothy 2:15 refers to those truths.

"Rightly dividing," and "handling aright" are two of the translations of the Greek word "orthotomounta." This is a form of "orthotomeo" which the lexicon defines: "to cut straight; to direct aright; to set forth truthfully without perversion, or distortion, 2 Timothy 2:15." Since the basic idea in the word is "cutting it straight," Paul may have been alluding to his work as a tent maker by using this word. (Acts 18:3.) He had to cut straight or properly the cloth out of which he made tents. It had to be cut so it would fit in his making tents.

Whether Paul alluded to cutting tent cloth or not, we are certain that the Holy Spirit meant in the words he gave him in 2 Timothy 2:15 that to properly handle the Bible we must interpret or "cut straight" every passage of Holy Scripture so that each passage "fits" every other passage. It is a gross violation of this holy hermeneutical principle to say a Bible passage means that which contradicts another passage or passages in the Bible!

Such gross mishandling and distorting and perversion of the word of God has for centuries been the cause of the teaching of many false and contradictory religious doctrines, and the cause of the origin of hundreds of denominational churches and religious organizations. Such a conglomeration of contradiction, conflict, and confusion has been the cause of much disgust with religion as well as the cause of much deception characterized by the attitude that it matters not what one's interpretation of the Bible is, or what one believes as long as he is sincere. Nothing could be further from the truth.

The great Bible scholar, Albert Barnes said many people use less sense and reasoning in their views about religion and the Bible than in any other area of their thinking or any other pursuit. It is obvious as one looks at and thinks about the condition of the religious world and all its confusion that what Mr. Barnes said it still very true. This condition is vastly separated from the condition of the unity of all those who would believe on and follow Jesus for which he prayed in John 17:20-23 which says, "I do not pray for these alone, but also for those who will believe in Me through their word; that they all may be one; as You, Father, are in Me, and I in You; that they also may be one in Us, that the world may believe that You sent Me. And the glory which You gave Me I have given them, that they may be one just as We are one: I in them, and You in Me; that they may be perfect in one, and that the world may know that You have sent Me, and have loved them as You have loved Me."

The Bible also stresses the unity for which Jesus prayed in the following New Testament passages.

"Now I urge you, brethren, note those who cause divisions and offenses, contrary to the doctrine which you learned, and avoid them." (Romans 16:17.)

"Now I plead with you, brethren, by the name of our Lord Jesus Christ, that you all speak the same thing, and that there be no divisions among you, but that you be perfectly joined together in the same mind and in the same judgment." (1 Corinthians 1:10.)

"I, therefore, the prisoner of the Lord, beseech you to walk worthy of the calling with which you were called, with all lowliness and gentleness, with longsuffering, bearing with one another in love, endeavoring to keep the unity of the Spirit in the bond of peace. There is one body and one Spirit, just as you were called in one hope of your calling; one Lord, one faith, one baptism; one God and Father of all, who is above all, and through all, and in you all." (Ephesians 4:1-6.)

"And being confident of this, I know that I shall remain and continue with you all for your progress and joy of faith, that your rejoicing for me may be more abundant in Jesus Christ by my coming to you again. Only let your conduct be worthy of the gospel of Christ, so that whether I come and see you or am absent, I may hear of your affairs, that you stand fast in one spirit, with one mind striving together for the faith of the gospel." (Philippians 1:25-27.)

Salvation By God's Grace

The Bible says much about the salvation of sinners by the grace of God, but it does not teach both salvation by God's grace alone, and salvation by God's grace and obedience to him. If one interprets Bible passages to teach that we can be saved by God's grace without obedience to him, that would not be "cutting it straight." To do so leaves the impression that some verses in Holy Scripture do not fit other verses in Holy Scripture which clearly teach that obedience to God is absolutely necessary to being saved by God's grace.

The word "grace" is not in the New Testament books of Matthew and Mark. It is in the book of Luke only one time, and that is Luke 2:40 where Luke wrote of Jesus, "And the Child grew and became strong in spirit, filled with wisdom; and the grace of God was upon Him." The word "grace" is in the Gospel of John only four times. "And the Word became flesh and dwelt among us, and we beheld His glory, the glory as of the only begotten of the Father, full of grace and truth. John bore witness of Him and cried out, saying, 'This was He of whom I said, He who comes after me is preferred before me, for He was before me.' And of his fullness we have all received, and grace for grace. For the law was given through Moses, but grace and truth came through Jesus Christ.'" (John 1:14-17)

The "fullness" of Christ and "grace for grace" of verse 16 are very significant. Paul wrote of Christ to the Christians in Colosse, "For in Him dwells all the fullness of the Godhead bodily; and you are complete in Him, who is the head of all principality and power. In Him you were also circumcised with the circumcision made without hands, by putting off the body of the sins of the flesh by the circumcision of Christ, buried with him in baptism, in which you also

177

were raised with Him through faith in the working of God, who raised Him from the dead." (Colossians 2:9-12.)

Observe that all "the fullness of the Godhead bodily" dwells in Christ. The New Testament teaches that "the Godhead bodily" consists of God the Father, God the Holy Spirit, and God the Son. The fullness of all three persons of Deity is in God the Son. All spiritual blessings available to human beings by the grace of God are available in Christ Jesus. "Blessed be the God and Father of our Lord Jesus Christ, who has blessed us with every spiritual blessing in the heavenly places in Christ." (Ephesians 1:3.) That is why Paul said, "And you are complete in Him." (Colossians 2:10.) Paul also made it clear that fullness and completeness are reached when we are spiritually circumcised with "the circumcision of Christ" when we are buried and raised in baptism. (Colossians 2:11,12.)

Paul also said the fullness that God has put in Christ is also in Christ's body which is His church. "Which He worked in Christ when He raised Him from the dead and seated Him at His right hand in the heavenly places, far above all principality and power and might and dominion, and every name that is named, not only in this age but also in that which is to come. And He put all things under His feet, and gave Him to be head over all things to the church, which is His body, the fullness of Him who fills all in all." (Ephesians 1:20-23.)

John emphasized all this greatness of Christ and all this fullness that is in Him when he said He is "full of grace and truth... and of His fullness have all we received, and grace for grace." (John 1:14,16.)

The "for" in "grace for grace" is the translation of the Greek preposition "anti" which means "against" or "upon." This is a difficult statement in the English. John evidently emphasized the abundance of the grace that is in Christ. Apparently he alluded to an abundance of some commodity; perhaps grain in bags stored in a large building with one bag or sack against another to illustrate the abundance of God's grace to save the lost. There is enough of it to save all the lost, but all the lost are not saved by it because some refuse to do what God requires in order to have His salvation by His grace.

This awesome truth is well expressed in Titus 2:11-15, "For the grace of God that brings salvation has appeared to all men, teaching us that, denying ungodliness and worldly lusts, we should live soberly, righteously, and godly in the present age, looking for the blessed hope and glorious appearing of our great God and Savior Jesus

Christ, who gave Himself for us, that He might redeem us from every lawless deed and purify for Himself His own special people, zealous for good works. Speak these things, exhort, and rebuke with all authority. Let no one despise you." This passage clearly states that "the grace of God that saves" saves by teaching us what not to do, and what to do, and by our living in such a manner that we look for the blessed hope of the coming of Christ our Savior by our being zealous of good works.

This all means when someone misuses a Bible passage, or Bible passages to say that salvation is by grace alone, he is not cutting those passages straight. The way he misuses such passages causes those passages not to fit or blend with other passages which teach that God's grace saves on certain conditions!

For an example, when one says baptism in water cannot be necessary to salvation because we are saved by God's grace. Some say this when someone quotes to them Acts 2:36-41 which says, "Therefore let all the house of Israel know assuredly that God has made this Jesus, whom you crucified, both Lord and Christ. Now when they heard this, they were cut to the heart, and said to Peter and the rest of the apostles, 'Men and brethren, what shall we do?' Then Peter said to them, 'Repent, and let every one of you be baptized in the name of Jesus Christ for the remission of sins; and you shall receive the gift of the Holy Spirit. For the promise is to you and to your children, and to all who are afar off, as many as the Lord our God will call. And with many other words he testified and exhorted them, saying, 'Be saved from this perverse generation. Then those who gladly received his word were baptized and that day about three thousand souls were added to them."

Had Peter not been speaking as the Spirit gave him utterance (Acts 2:4) he might have answered those who were cut to the heart, "There is nothing you can do, because you are too mean and corrupt and sinful. I have just told you that you have with wicked hands crucified the Son of God (Acts 2:23) and that God has made that same Jesus you crucified both Lord and Christ." (Acts 2:36.) Peter could have added, "You are so mean that there is no hope for you! You are going to be annihilated; you are going to the eternal regions of woe where the eternal piercings of the undying worms will torture you forever." But grace came! God announced through Peter His immeasurable favor upon them when he said, "Repent you and be baptized every one of you in the name of Jesus Christ, for the remission of sins and you shall receive the gift of the Holy Spirit." Those who accepted Peter's answer gladly received it and were baptized to be saved by God's grace! They did not argue about baptism or try to avoid being immersed on the grounds that they could be saved by grace without it! There is no case in the New Testament where anyone argued about water baptism and tried to prove it was not essential to salvation in Christ.

The grace of God is magnified by what the New Testament teaches about those who are out of Christ and lost in their sins. If such lost people are aware of how bad their sins are before God, they can easily see how indeed abundant God's grace is when he promises their sins will be remitted or blotted out when they are baptized into Christ (Romans 6:3) and for the remission of their sins! (Acts 2:38.)

Even the precious grace of God, his overwhelming and unmerited favor, is misrepresented when preachers and others argue against baptism being essential on the grounds that God's grace saves without baptism. The command of God to be baptized to be saved is a part of the gospel which God gave to the lost world by his grace! It is a part of "the gospel of the grace of God." (Acts 20:24.) It is a part of "the word of His grace." (Acts 14:3.)

Those who teach that God saves those out of Christ by His grace without baptism do not "cut it straight." They do not "handle aright the word of truth." They make the word of God seem to contradict itself.

After the apostle Peter wrote about the return of Jesus Christ and the destruction of the heavens and the earth, he wrote: "Therefore, beloved, looking forward to these things, be diligent to be found by Him in peace, without spot and blameless; and account that the longsuffering of our Lord is salvation – as also our beloved brother Paul, according to the wisdom given to him, has written to you, as also in all his epistles, speaking in them of these things, in which are some things hard to understand, which those who are untaught and unstable twist to their own destruction, as they do also the rest of the Scriptures. You therefore, beloved, since you know these things beforehand, beware lest you also fall from your own steadfastness, being led away with the error of the wicked; but grow in the grace and knowledge of our Lord and Savior Jesus Christ. To Him be the glory both now and forever. Amen." (2 Peter 3:14-16.)

This passage is from the New King James Version. The King James Version has "wrest" where "twist" is in the NKJV. The Greek word for "twist" and "wrest" is the word "streblousin." This is a form of the word that means: a windlass, a wrench; instrument of torture (rack). The verb form means to distort the limbs of a human body on a rack. Hence the word came to mean distortion and perversion.

Apparently, in ancient times, those accused of crimes were put on torture racks that were equipped with a windlass and ropes arranged so the person's body could be stretched and distorted to get him to confess his crime.

People still wrest the scriptures as holy and as precious as they are. They wrest and stretch and twist them out of shape and use the distorted and perverted doctrines to deceive.

People not only wrest the scriptures, they also "rest" them. They rarely ever read the Bible; they let it rest in a drawer or on a shelf. In fact some seem to think the Bible is a dry book just because it may have dust on it. But he who thinks the Bible is a dry book is all wet!

What Peter wrote about some twisting the Holy Scriptures to their own destruction is the same thing as saying that some do not "cut straight" or handle aright the word of God!

Questions And Discussion Points

What does "hermeneutics" mean?

What was the difference in the Greek and Roman gods?

How many times is the word "grace" in Matthew's and Mark's books?

Discuss "for" in John 1:16.

What does the grace of God that saves teach us? How?

Explain why Acts 2:38 is a demonstration of God's grace.

What does "wrest" or "twist" mean in 2 Peter 3:16?

How can a person "rest" the Holy Scriptures?

Chapter Twenty-six

OTHER EXAMPLES OF HOW TO "CUT STRAIGHT" THE WORD OF GOD

Perhaps there is nothing pertaining to the right interpretation of the Bible that is more important than "cutting it straight" as explained in the previous chapter, and also in this the final chapter of this book.

How Does God Give Repentance And Also Command It?

Several years ago I was in a Sunday morning Bible class being taught by a young brother. He did not "cut it straight" as he talked about repentance. He taught the Calvinistic view that God arbitrarily gives repentance to sinners so they can be saved.

The New Testament does say in several passages that God gives repentance. "But Peter and the other apostles answered and said: 'We ought to obey God rather than men. The God of our fathers raised up Jesus whom you murdered by hanging on a tree. Him God has exalted to His right hand to be Prince and Savior, to give repentance to Israel and forgiveness of sins.'" (Acts 5:29-31.)

"When they heard these things they became silent; and they glorified God, saying, 'Then God has also granted to the Gentiles repentance to life." (Acts 11:18.)

"In humility correcting those who are in opposition, if God perhaps will grant them repentance, so that they may know the truth." (2 Timothy 2:25.)

There are New Testament passages which show that God commands repentance, and that some who should have repented did not. To "cut it straight" and to "handle aright the word of truth," our hermeneutical handling of it should direct us to show that the passages which say God gives or grants repentance, and the passages, which show that God commands it, are in perfect harmony. The following passages are some of the latter.

"Then He began to rebuke the cities in which most of His mighty works had been done, because they did not repent: 'Woe to you, Chorazin! Woe to you, Bethsaida! For if the mighty works which were done in you had been done in Tyre and Sidon, they would have repented long ago in sackcloth and ashes.'" (Matthew 11:20,21.)

"John came baptizing in the wilderness and preaching a baptism of repentance for the remission of sins." (Mark 1:4.)

"When Jesus heard it, He said to them, 'Those who are well have no need of a physician, but those who are sick. I did not come to call the righteous, but sinners, to repentance.'" (Mark 2:17.)

"I say to you that likewise there will be more joy in heaven over one sinner who repents than over ninety-nine just persons who need no repentance." (Luke 15:7.)

"Now I rejoice, not that you were made sorry, but that your sorrow led to repentance. For you were made sorry in a goodly manner, that you might suffer loss from us in nothing. For godly sorrow produces repentance leading to salvation, not to be regretted; but the sorrow of the world produces death." (2 Corinthians 7:9,10.)

"For I fear lest, when I come, I shall not find you such as I wish, and that I shall be found by you such as you do not wish; lest there be contentions, jealousies, outbursts of wrath, selfish ambitions, backbitings, whisperings, conceits, tumults; and lest, when I come again, my God will humble me among you, and I shall mourn for many who have sinned before and have not repented of the uncleanness, fornication, and lewdness which they have practiced." (2 Corinthians 12:20,21.)

"The Lord is not slack concerning His promise, as some count slackness, but is longsuffering toward us, not willing that any should perish but that all should come to repentance." (2 Peter 3:9.)

When "cut straight," or rightly handled with the right hermeneutical principle, the scriptures presented in the foregoing on God's giving or granting repentance, and the ones which make it obvious God commands sinners to repent, all obviously mean that God gives or grants repentance in the sense that He allows sinners the opportunity to come to repentance and at the same time commands them to repent. The Scriptures teach that God granted some the opportunity to repent who refused to repent!

A good example of this is what Jesus said to the people of Jerusalem recorded in Matthew 23:37, which says, "O Jerusalem, Jerusalem, the one who kills the prophets and stones those who are sent to her! How often I wanted to gather your children together, as a hen gathers her chicks under her wings, but you were not willing!"

Jesus had given those people the opportunity to repent many times, and they refused his offers because they had the wrong attitude. We determine our eternal destiny by our attitude!

Another example is in Acts 13:45, 46 which tells what Paul and Barnabas told some Jews in Antioch of Pisidia. "But when the Jews saw the multitudes, they were filled with envy; and contradicting and blaspheming, they opposed the things spoken by Paul. Then Paul and Barnabas grew bold and said, 'It was necessary that the word of God should be spoken to you first; but since you reject it, and judge yourselves unworthy of everlasting life; behold, we turn to the Gentiles.'" Those Jews were also given the opportunity to repent, but they refused to do so and judged themselves unworthy of eternal life. They could have become some of God's elect which means they could have believed in Christ as the Son of God, turned from their sins in repentance, confessed their faith in Christ and been baptized into Christ for the forgiveness of their sins. (Acts 2:38.)

The Vine And The Branches

Even before Jesus established or built His church on the first day of Pentecost following His resurrection, He used parables, analogies, and other methods to illustrate and emphasize traits of the church and truths regarding it. The following is an example.

"I am the true vine, and My Father is the vinedresser. Every branch in Me that does not bear fruit He takes away; and every branch that bears fruit He prunes, that it may bear more fruit. You are already clean because of the word which I have spoken to you. Abide in Me, and I in you. As the branch cannot bear fruit of itself, unless it abides in the vine, neither can you, unless you abide in Me. I am the vine, you are the branches. He who abides in Me, and I in him, bears much fruit; for without Me you can do nothing. If anyone does not abide in Me, he is cast out as a branch and is withered; and they gather them and throw them into the fire, and they are burned." (John 15:1-6.)

Many people have misused, and have not "cut straight" what our precious Savior said in His analogy of the vine and the branches. In their attempts to justify the massive amounts of divisions in the conglomeration of conflicts and confusion in what is called Christendom, they have contended that the branches in the analogy represent different denominations in the divided religious world of all churches that claim allegiance to Christ. With this misunderstanding in mind, let everyone consider the facts and observations that follow.

1. One reason we can know that Jesus did not speak of religious division in His vine and branches sermon, is because a vine and its

branches illustrate unity, not division. All the bark of a vine and its branches is the same. All its leaves are the same. All its sap is the same. All its fruit is the same. This is unity indeed. No one expects to find a grapevine that has grapes, blackberries, strawberries, plums, peaches, cucumbers, watermelons, and other fruits growing on it!

2. If Jesus taught religious division in John 15 in the vine and its branches analogy, He contradicted Himself in His prayer to His Father in John 17 when he prayed, "I do not pray for these alone, but also for those who will believe in Me through their word; that they all may be one, as You, Father, are in Me, and I in You; that they also may be one in Us, that the world may believe that You sent Me. And the glory which You gave Me I have given them, that they may be one just as We are one: I in them, and You in Me; that they may be made perfect in one, and that the world may know that You have sent Me, and have loved them as You have loved Me." (John 17:20-23.)

Jesus had just prayed for His apostles, when He said, "I do not pray for these alone." Then He prayed for the unity of all those who would believe on Him through, or by means of the word or message of the apostles. In the same prayer He had already said to the Father that He had given the Father's word to them. This means that the Father's word is the means by which all those who believe on Jesus can be one as Jesus and the Father are one. This is the highest ideal for unity or oneness there is.

In one of my debates my opponent argued that there is only one person in the Godhead. He misused Jesus' statement, "I and my Father are one." (John 10:30.) I was 28 years old, and I would respond now, about 50 years later, as I did then to such a wresting of Scripture. To say Jesus meant that He and His Father are the same person is not "cutting straight" what Jesus meant when He said, "I and my Father are one," because Jesus also said, "My Father is greater than I." (John 14:28.) I explained in that debate if the Father and Jesus are one in the sense of their being one person, then the Father could not be greater than Jesus.

I also explained in that debate that Jesus prayed to the Father and He was not praying to Himself! He prayed that all those who would believe on Him would be one as He and the Father are one. I asked my opponent if Jesus prayed that all those who believed on Him would be one mammoth disciple. My opponent "observed the passover" on that question!

Because of the unity of His followers for which Jesus prayed in John chapter seventeen, we can be certain that those who say Jesus taught denominational division in the analogy of the vine and the branches in John chapter fifteen are not "cutting straight" what He taught in that analogy. They do not handle aright, or rightly divide, the word of truth!

3. If Jesus taught religious division in the analogy of the vine and the branches, He contradicted what the Holy Spirit plainly said through the apostle Paul about religious unity and oneness.

"Now I plead with you, brethren, by the name of our Lord Jesus Christ, that you all speak the same thing, and that there be no divisions among you, but that you be perfectly joined together in the same mind and in the same judgment. For it has been declared to me concerning you, by brethren, by those of Chloe's household, that there are contentions among you." (1 Corinthians 1:10,11.) Paul then specified how the Corinthian church was divided into four groups. In chapter three he told them that because there was envy, strife, and divisions among them, they were carnal and not spiritual. He did not say that in their divided state they demonstrated what Jesus meant in His analogy of the vine and the branches!

4. Paul did not contradict what Jesus said in His analogy of the vine and the branches in what he wrote to the church of Christ in Ephesus in the following.

"I therefore, the prisoner of the Lord, beseech you to have a walk worthy of the calling with which you were called, with all lowliness and gentleness, with longsuffering, bearing with one another in love, endeavoring to keep the unity of the Spirit in the bond of peace. There is one body and one Spirit, just as you were called in one hope of your calling; one Lord, one faith, one baptism; one God and Father of all, who is above all, and through all, and in you all." (Ephesians 4:1-6.)

The oneness and "unity of the Spirit taught in the foregoing Scripture make it ridiculous for anyone to say Jesus taught religious division in the analogy of the vine and the branches. Those who say Jesus did teach division in that analogy do not "cut straight" or handle aright the word of truth. Notice that Paul told the church in Ephesus to endeavor to keep the unity of the Spirit in the bond of peace. The word "endeavoring" in the text is a translation of the Greek word "spoudazontes" which is also translated "being eager."

The word is a form of "speudo" which, according to the lexicons, means a sense of urgency; to be in earnest about; to be bent upon or determined; to strive for earnestly.

When there is unity in the church the members should work diligently and earnestly to keep it! It is easy to lose it! Notice in Paul's charge that endeavoring to keep unity involves our walking "with all lowliness and gentleness, with longsuffering, bearing with one another in love."

Not only does the New Testament clearly teach that Christ's people who are His church are to be united, it also stresses the importance of keeping or maintaining the unity of the Spirit. Obviously that unity is the unity that results from following what the Spirit says in the New Testament. This is the same as what Jesus meant in that prayer when He prayed all would be one through the word of the apostles which was the word of the Father which Jesus said He gave to His apostles.

In view of all this it is sad and lamentable that anyone says that Jesus taught religious division and denominationalism in His great lesson on the vine and the branches.

5. If "branch" and "branches" in John chapter fifteen means "denomination" and "denominations" it would be all right to put these words in the text to replace "branch" and "branches." Try that! When you get to verse six, you will make Jesus say, "If anyone does not abide in Me, he is cast forth as a <u>denomination</u> and is withered; and they gather them and throw them in the fire and they are burned."

That will not work, will it? A denomination is not an "anyone: nor a "he."

Some have asked me, "Of what church are you a member?" My response has been, "I am a member of the Lord's church." Then I would be asked, "to what branch of the church do you belong?" Then I respond, "I do not belong to a <u>branch</u>, I am a branch!" The Lord did not tell each of His followers to abide in a branch. Instead He taught that each of His followers is a branch, and each branch is to abide in Him who is the vine!

6. Some call attention to "the seven churches of Asia" of Revelation chapters 1, 2, and 3 in an attempt to show that Jesus taught denominational division in His lesson on the vine and the branches. Doing this is another case of not "cutting it straight," or not handling aright the Lord's word. The seven churches of Asia were not seven

different denominations, but they were seven congregations of the Lord's church.

Notice that in chapter two and three of Revelation, reference is made to; (1) "the church of Ephesus"; (2) "the church in Smyrna"; (3) "the church in Pergamos"; (4) "the church in Thyatira"; (5) "the church in Sardis"; (6) "the church in Philadelphia"; and (7) "the church of the Laodiceans."

Conclusion

Some might say I need to quit teaching what the New Testament teaches about unity, because there is too much division for me to do any good. For me or anyone else to do this would indeed be disastrous just like my quitting teaching what the Bible teaches on what proper morals are because there is so much immorality!

The Bible is not the cause of religious confusion and division. Not cutting the word of God straight is the cause.

Questions And Discussion Points

Does the Bible say God gives repentance?

Does God command repentance?

Discuss Matthew 23:37.

Can people judge themselves unworthy of eternal life?

Does "branches" in John 15 mean churches? Explain.

Discuss John 17:20-23.

Discuss 1 Corinthians 1:10,11.

Discuss Ephesians 4:1-6.

Bibliography

Alexander, Archibald, *The Canon Of The Old And New Testaments* published 1826.

Archer, Gleason L., *A Survey Of Old Testament Introduction*

A Survey Of Old Testament Introduction, Moody Press, Chicago, 1994, page 81

Alexander's Evidence of Christianity

Arndt, Gingrich, Bauer, and Danker., *A Greek-English Lexicon Of The New Testament, and Other Christian Literature* (Also see *The Analytical Greek Lexicon* by Harper Brothers and Samuel Bagster and Sons.)

Burgon, Dean, *The Last Twelve Verses Of Mark*

Campbell, Alexander, *The Christian Preacher's Companion, Or The Gospel Facts Sustained By The Testimony Of Unbelieving Jews And Pagans.*

Can I Trust My Bible: Important Questions Often Asked About The Bible, With Some Answers By Eight Evangelical Scholars; Moody Bible Institute of Chicago, 1966

Canon Of Scripture

Collett, Sidney, *All About The Bible*, Fleming H. Revel Co

Collins, Dr. John J., professor of Old Testament at Yale University, and Dr. Robert A. Kugler of Gonzaga University in Spokane, Washington are the editors of a book entitled: *Religion In The Dead Sea Scrolls*

Curtis, Helena, *Biology*, Worth Publishers, Inc., Second Printing, August 1979

The Dead Sea Scrolls After Forty Years is the title of a book copyrighted in 1991 by the Biblical Archaeology Society, 3000 Connecticut Avenue, N.W. in Washington D.C

Durant, Will, *The Story of Civilization*, Volume 3, Christ and Caesar

Gaussen, S. R. L., *Theopneusty, Or The Plenary Inspiration Of The Holy Scriptures.*
It was translated from French into English by Edward Norris Kirk. Gaussen was a professor of theology in Geneva, Switzerland.

Green, F. M., *The Life And Times of John F. Rowe*, published in 1899.

Green, Dr. W. H., *International Standard Bible Encyclopedia*, Vol. 1

Hamilton, Floyd, *The Basis of Christian Faith.*

Hardeman's Tabernacle Sermons, Vol. IV

Hickman, Cleveland, Larry Roberts, and Frances Hickman, *Integrated Principles of Zoology*, Seventh Edition, Times Mirror/Mosby College Publishing, 1984.

International Standard Bible Encyclopedia, Vol. I

Introduction To The Old Testament, published by William B. Eerdmans in Grand Rapids, MI., 1971.

Jastrow, Dr. Robert, *Until The Sun Dies.*

Leach, Charles, *Our Bible: How We Got It*, Moody Press, 1898

Lightfoot, Neil, *How We Got The Bible*, Baker Book House, 1963

Matthew Henry's Commentary on the Bible, Volume IV.

M'Clintock, Dr. John, and Dr. James Strong, entitled *Cyclopedia of Biblical, Theological and Ecclesiastical Literature.*

McGarvey, J. W., *The Authorship of Deuteronomy* published in 1902 by the Standard Publishing Company of Cincinnati, OH.

McGarvey, J.W., *Commentary On Matthew and Mark*

McGarvey, J.W., *Evidences of Christianity* published in 1886 by Standard Publishing Company in Cincinnati, OH.

McGarvey, J.W., *Sermons Delivered In Louisville, Kentucky*, page 12; Christian Standard Publishing Co., 1984

Metzger, Dr., *The Early Versions Of The New Testament.*

Metzger, Bruce M., *The Test Of The New Testament*, Second Edition, Oxford University Press

Meyer, Heinrich A.W., *Critical And Exegitical Handbook On The Gospels Of Mark And Luke,* First printed in 1883. Reprinted in 1980, by Alpha Publications, Winona Lake, IN.

Nelson's New Illustrated Bible Dictionary

New Testament Manuscript Studies, The University Of Chicago Press, 1950

New World Dictionary of the American Language

Paley, William, *A View Of The Evidences Of Christianity*, page 34. This book was republished in 1952 by my old friend George DeHoff

Pulpit Commentary, Volume 14

Russell, W. J., *New Testament Christianity*, Vol., II, Edited by Z. T. Sweeney; pages 358, 359; 1926

Schiffman, Lawrence H., *Reclaiming The Dead Sea Scrolls* is the name of a book written by and published by Doubleday Company in 1995

Schmucker, S. S. publisher of a two volume set of books entitled *Biblical Theology*. My copy of Volume 1 was published in 1826. Schmucker's works are translations of writings of two German scholars, Dr. Theophilus Christian Storr, and Dr. C. C. Flatt. Dr. Storr was a professor of theology in the University of Tübingen.

Shanks, Dr. Hershel, *The Dead Sea Scrolls After Forty Years*

Smith, James, *History of The Christian Church*, page 58. My copy was published in 1835.

Smith, James, *The Christian's Defence,* 1843.

Stoughton, John, *Matthew Henry's Bible Commentary,* Volume I.

Thiessen, Dr. Henry Clarence, Chairman of the faculty of the Graduate School of Wheaton College in Wheaton, IL. *Introduction To The New Testament.*

Weizmar, Steve, *Archaeologists Uncover Ancient Graves Near Site Where Dead Sea Scrolls Found,* Associated Press news story the July 27, 2001 edition of the *Times Daily* in Florence, AL.

Wise, Michael, Martin Abegg, Jr., and Edward Cook, *Dead Sea Scrolls – A New Translation – Translated And With Commentary*, published in 1996 by Harper San Francisco.

Wisse, Frederic, *The Text Of The New Testament In Contemporary Research*, Edited by Bart D. Erhman and Michael W. Holes; William B. Eerdmans Publishing Company; 1995.

The Works Of William E. Channing, D.D., page 229; Boston, American Unitarian Association, 1877.

The Works of Josephus, The S.S. Scranton Company, 1919

Young, Dr. E. J., *The Canon of the Old Testament, in Revelation and the Bible*

Young, Dr. Edward J., *An Introduction To The Old Testament*